The Dream
and the Struggle

Separate but not Equal

POLARIS

A new direction in nonfiction.

The Dream
and the Struggle

Separate
but not
Equal

Jim Haskins

SCHOLASTIC INC.   NEW YORK · TORONTO · LONDON · AUCKLAND · SYDNEY
MEXICO CITY · NEW DELHI · HONG KONG

No part of this publication may be reproduced in whole or in part, or stored in
a retrieval system, or transmitted in any form or by any means, electronic, mechanical,
photocopying, recording, or otherwise, without written permission of the publisher.
For information regarding permission, write to Scholastic Inc.,
Attention: Permissions Department, 555 Broadway, New York, NY 10012.

ISBN 0-590-45911-2

12 11 10 9 8 7 6 5 4 3   2 3 4 5 6/0

Printed in the U.S.A.   40

First Scholastic paperback printing, January 2001

"Education is the development of power and ideal. Our children have a right to know, to think, to aspire." —W. E. B. Du Bois, August 1906

I am grateful to Kathy Benson for her help. A special thank-you to my editor and friend, Ann Reit.

To the memory of Thurgood Marshall

CONTENTS

1.

Little Rock, Arkansas

September 3, 1957, was unlike any other opening day at Central High School in Little Rock, Arkansas. For on that day, as part of court-ordered desegregation, nine black teenagers entered the previously all-white institution. Elizabeth Eckford was among the nine. She was one of the high-achieving students chosen by the National Association for the Advancement of Colored People (NAACP) for this groundbreaking event. Like the other eight students, she was from a good family and had a strong religious upbringing. The NAACP knew all too well that the first black students at Central High would have to be exceptional human beings with unimpeachable characters and the faith and strength to be "firsts."

In addition to Elizabeth Eckford, the students were Minnijean Brown, Ernest Green, Thelma Mothershed, Melba Patillo, Gloria Ray, Terrence Roberts, Jefferson Thomas, and Carlotta Walls. In the weeks before the start of school, the nine attended countless meetings at which the plans to

Separate But Not Equal

Central High School in Little Rock, Arkansas, and six of the nine black students who were admitted. Top row (left to right): Gloria Ray, Terrence Roberts, Melba Patillo. Bottom row (left to right): Jefferson Thomas, Carlotta Walls, Thelma Mothershed.

desegregate Central High were discussed and at which the students were counseled about what to expect. The NAACP knew that this was a crucial event in the campaign to desegregate the schools in the South; they wanted nothing to go wrong.

Just before opening day, Arkansas governor Orval Faubus announced that he would call in the National Guard to prevent the nine black students from entering Central High. On the night of September 2, Mrs. Daisy Bates, head of the local NAACP chapter, Wiley Branton, an attorney from the national NAACP, and others decided that the students should all meet in one place near Central High the following morning so they could go to the high school as a group. But Elizabeth Eckford did not have a phone, and there was no way to reach her. The following morning, in a starched dress and carrying an armload of notebooks, sunglasses hiding the fear in her eyes, Elizabeth Eckford stood in front of Central High and faced a line of uniformed and helmeted National Guardsmen cradling rifles in their arms. She had no idea what door she was supposed to enter. When she spied what seemed to be a break in the line of uniformed men, the five-foot-tall girl approached it. The National Guardsmen closed ranks to shut her out. She walked farther along the line and tried another opening. Again, the soldiers closed ranks.

A huge crowd of whites lined the sidewalk across the street from Central High. They chanted, "Two, four, six, eight, we ain't gonna integrate!" and shouted, "Nigger, go home! Nigger, go back where you belong!" Each time Elizabeth Eckford was shut out by the National Guardsmen, the crowd hooted and cheered, shouted, stomped, and whistled in triumph.

Frightened and alone, desperately looking for a friendly face and finding none, wondering what had happened to Mrs. Bates, Mr. Branton, and the other students, Elizabeth decided the best thing to do was go home. She made her way to a nearby bus stop amid shouts of "Get her, get the nigger out of here!" Elizabeth sat with her back ramrod straight, numb to the abuse, praying for the bus to come. When it did, she was barely able to walk up the steps of the vehicle, she was shaking so violently. But she made it and, as the bus pulled away, she wondered how she could ever summon up the courage to return to Central High.

But she did return. It took action by the president of the United States, Dwight D. Eisenhower, to secure the admittance of the nine black students to Central High. He ordered federal troops to Little Rock to ensure that the students would be admitted and, once inside, not harmed.

President Eisenhower ordered federal troops to escort the students to school.

How could this have happened in the United States of America? How, in this nation founded on the principle that all men are created equal, could so much hatred have been directed at one young girl who simply wanted to go to the school of her choice?

It happened because of history — a long, shameful story of America's denying African Americans the most basic human rights. That history cannot be changed. But laws can be changed, and so can the minds and hearts of people; and with those changes, a new chapter of history can be written — a prouder history about trying to overcome past injustices and living up to the promise of equal opportunity for all. This book is about the struggle of African Americans for equal rights to education, perhaps the most important right an American can enjoy.

2.

In Colonial Times

Knowledge is power; that has long been understood. In seventeenth-century England, the Puritans declared that learning was power, to the horror of conservatives, who were against the education of the working class. It would "teach them to despise their lot in life . . . instead of teaching them subordination, it would render them fractious and refractory. . . . It would enable them to read seditious pamphlets, and . . . would render them insolent to their superiors."

Those same words could have been spoken by most of the slaveholders in North America in arguments against the education of slaves. If slaves could read and write, they could forge traveling passes and therefore escape to freedom. If slaves could read, they might get hold of antislavery literature and be inspired to protest their condition. Learning would make slaves discontented.

In the earliest years of European settlement of this country, slavery was not the harsh chattel system that it later became. African slaves were comparatively few in number; and there is considerable evidence that they were treated similarly to white indentured servants, although white indentured servants could eventually work off their indenture and become free. Farms, which employed the majority of slaves, were small; and there was no huge cash crop, as cotton would later become, that required the labor of thousands. There was considerable contact between whites and blacks, slave or free. And in areas where education was stressed for whites, blacks sometimes also benefited.

In those early days there were no public schools. What few schools existed were usually

A Colonial schoolroom scene

associated with churches or religious groups, for Christianity required knowledge of the Bible. Those who believed that slaves should be Christianized also believed that they should be taught to read the Bible. From earliest times, it was a religious group, the Quakers, that was in the forefront of efforts to educate blacks. The Quakers, more formally known as the Society of Friends, were founded in England in the middle of the seventeenth century. They believed that religion was a personal matter and that no priest or rite was needed to establish communion between the soul and God. The group was derisively called Quakers because of the way its adherents shivered or "quaked" when they felt the power of God in them. Many Quakers emigrated to the English colonies in North America seeking freedom to practice their faith. The colony of Pennsylvania was established by Quakers. In the late 1600s, groups of Quakers openly protested the prohibition against education of slaves as un-Christian and opposed to the nature of man.

In other colonies, the Church of England sometimes conducted the instruction of slaves. In New York in 1704, a school for blacks was opened under the direction of one Elias Neau. But the school was forced to close eight years later, when Neau was accused of abetting slave uprisings.

Another colony in North America that emphasized the education of blacks was Louisiana. The strong Catholic culture of its Spanish founders and later French colonizers stressed education for all. In 1734, a group of Ursuline nuns established a school for blacks in the city of New Orleans.

But such educational opportunities for blacks in North America were few. Even in areas that stressed education, the prevailing attitude was that blacks were by nature inferior and unable to learn. Despite the odds against them, a few blacks in Colonial America managed to achieve an education. They served as role models for other blacks and exposed as untrue the belief that blacks were intellectually inferior to whites.

One of the most famous examples was Benjamin Banneker, born free in Baltimore County, Maryland, in 1731. Educated by Quakers, Banneker proved to be gifted in mathematics and science. In 1754, at the age of twenty-four, he built a clock that not only told the time of day but also struck the hour. It is believed to be the first clock made in the United States. When, after the War of Independence, a site along the Potomac River was selected for the new nation's capital, Washington, D.C., President George Washington selected Banneker as part of the planning commission to lay out the new

Benjamin Banneker's
PENNSYLVANIA, DELAWARE, MARY-
LAND, AND VIRGINIA
.ALMANAC,
FOR THE
YEAR of our LORD 1795;
Being the Third after Leap-Year.

BANNAKER.

PHILADELPHIA:
Printed for WILLIAM GIBBONS, Cherry Street

The title page of Benjamin Banneker's Almanac

city. "I accepted this honor with great pride," Banneker later said, "not for myself but for my race."

In 1791, Banneker compiled an almanac, a table or calendar of days and months with astronomical information for each. The phases of the moon, the times of high and low tides, the best planting dates, and other useful information were also included. That first almanac was handwritten. Seeking a publisher and hoping to find support for his almanac, Banneker sent a copy to Thomas Jefferson, who was then secretary of state. Jefferson wrote to Banneker: "No body wishes more than I do to see such proofs as you exhibit, that nature has given our black brethren, talents equal to those of the other colors of men, and that the appearance of a want of them is owing merely to the degraded condition of their existence.... I considered it as a document to which your whole color had a right for their justification against the doubts which have been entertained of them."

By the following year, Banneker had found a publisher, and the 1792 *Benjamin Banneker's Pennsylvania, Delaware, Virginia, and Maryland Almanack and Ephemeris* was typeset and printed. Banneker would publish a new almanac every year until 1802. He died in 1806.

Another early example of an educated African American was the slave Phillis Wheatley, who was born in Africa, probably in Senegal, and captured by slavers when she was about six. When Susannah Wheatley, wife of a prosperous tailor named John Wheatley, saw her up for sale in a Boston slave market in 1761, the little girl was losing her front baby teeth. Susannah Wheatley fell in love with the little girl and, instead of putting her to work as a domestic servant, determined to rear her as her own daughter. In less than a year and a half in the Wheatley household, Phillis, as Susannah Wheatley named her, had learned English and could read the entire Bible. In 1765, she wrote her first letter.

Phillis Wheatley was fourteen when she wrote her first poem.

Wheatley wrote her first poem in 1767, at the age of fourteen, and saw another poem published three years later when she was seventeen. She was the first slave, first black, and second woman to publish a poem in the United States. The following year, her poem was published in a book of poetry in England. In 1772, she gathered what she felt was her best work and saw it published as *Poems on Various Subjects, Religious and Moral*. Her verses contained many references to the reading she had done. Although Wheatley never attended a school, she read widely and studied Latin, geography, and history.

In 1778, Wheatley married John Peters, a Bostonian who had started out as a grocer and then later read law to plead the cause of blacks, using the name Dr. Peters. She gave birth to three children, two of whom died. Life was a struggle. Her husband was jailed for debts he owed, and Phillis scrubbed and washed in a boardinghouse to support herself and her one surviving child. She had suffered from asthma since childhood, and she died at the age of thirty-one in 1784.

Still another early example of an educated African American was Paul Cuffe. Born in 1759, he was the seventh of ten children of Ruth Moses, a Wampanoag Indian woman and Cuffe Slocum, who had been born in Africa and brought to North America as a slave, and who had purchased his freedom from his master in Dartmouth, Massachusetts. Paul was only thirteen when his father died, and he scarcely knew the letters of the alphabet. But with the help of a tutor he learned to read and write. When the land his father had left him proved worthless, he went to sea, shipping out on a whaler bound for the Gulf of Mexico. During his third voyage, in 1776, the Revolutionary War broke out, and his ship was captured by the British. Cuffe spent three months in a New York prison and was then released. It was hazardous to go to sea during the war, and Cuffe found himself unable to make a living. Still, he was expected to pay taxes. In 1780, he and his brother John and five other free blacks petitioned the colony of Massachusetts for relief from taxation, citing their distressed financial condition. But the brothers were jailed for nonpayment of taxes. The following spring they continued to pursue their cause, putting the issue before a town meeting in Taunton, Connecticut, where they had been jailed.

Because he was educated, Paul Cuffe was keenly aware that one reason behind the revolt of the colonies against England was the charge of "no taxation without representation," that the colonies were expected to pay taxes to England even though they had no say in how the English government was conducted. The Cuffes demanded a vote as to "whether all free Negroes and molattoes shall have the same Privileges . . . as the white People have Respecting Places of profit, choosing of officers and the Like together with all other Privileges in all cases . . . or that we have Reliefe granted us Joyntly from Taxation . . ." The Cuffes finally had to pay the taxes they owed; but they courageously and determinedly fought for the same rights for which the white colonists were fighting the Revolution.

After the war, Cuffe married Alice Pequit, a woman of the Wampanoags, the same Native American group to which his mother belonged, and went back into shipping in partnership with his brother-in-law. They built ever larger vessels. By the time he was fifty years old, Captain Paul Cuffe owned a small fleet of ships. He used some of his profits to benefit the town of Westport, Connecticut, where he had settled. He built a schoolhouse for Westport with his own money on his own land and then donated both land and building "freely . . . to the use of the public." In 1808, he became a formal member of the Society of Friends and paid for half the cost of building a new Quaker meetinghouse in Westport.

The sense of outrage over the "evil of one

brother professor making merchandise of and holding his brother in bondage" and the failure of the new United States of America to live up to the promise of equality for all caused Cuffe in his later years to decide that the best course for freed slaves was to return to Africa, their ancestral land. In the fall of 1810, he sailed one of his ships with a crew of nine black seamen for Sierra Leone. There, he stayed three months, taking notes on its possibilities as a home for blacks from America. He made another trip to the country and then, in 1815, set sail on the *Traveller* with thirty-eight black emigrants and a cargo of supplies to get them started in their new home. Cuffe's health failed shortly after that and he died two years later, in October 1817. His dreams of a nation of black emigrants from America would be carried forth by others and bear fruit in the settling of Liberia by African-American freedmen in 1821. But there would never be a wholesale exodus of free blacks from the United States. As a group of free people of color in Richmond, Virginia, protested in January 1817, they preferred to be "colonized in the most remote corner of the land of our nativity, to being exiled" in Africa.

3.

The New Nation — The South

By the time independence from England had been won, and the thirteen colonies united to form a new nation, the United States of America, the laws of Virginia, Maryland, and the other colonies of the upper South had become harsher with respect to slaves. After the Revolution, the newly independent nation began to expand by adding new states; some of these states adopted the same harsh measures. Laws called slave codes were passed that prohibited slaves from marrying, traveling without special passes, and learning to read and write. These laws were meant to deny a sense of self-destiny to the slaves. They were also an attempt to forestall slaves' efforts to escape. There are stories of literate slaves aiding their own or others' escapes by writing travel passes or forging freedom documents.

South Carolina and Georgia led the way in repressing slave literacy. In some localities, it was a crime even to sell writing materials to slaves. In the 1830s, a series of slave revolts resulted in even more repressive legislation.

Despite the prohibitions against education, some determined slaves learned to read. Josiah Henson was one remarkable case. Born in Charles County, Maryland, in 1789, he was owned by three different masters before he managed to escape from slavery. One of those masters beat him with a stake, breaking his arm and perhaps both shoulder blades and maiming him for life. In 1830, he and his family, including four children, managed to escape to Canada and freedom. Once he had settled his family in their new home, Henson turned his attention to his fellow fugitives. In 1842, he helped to found the Dawn Institute, where fugitive slaves were taught trades so they could support themselves and their families in Canada.

Henson learned to read in Canada. In his autobiography, he explained: "It was, and has been ever since, a great comfort to me to have made this acquisition; though it has made me comprehend better the terrible abyss of ignorance in which I had been plunged all my previous life. It made me also feel more deeply and bitterly the oppression under which I had toiled and groaned; but the crushing and cruel nature of which I had not appreciated, till I found out, in some slight degree, from what I had been debarred. At the same time it made me more anxious than before to do something for the rescue and the elevation of those who were suffering the same evils I had endured, and who did not know how degraded and ignorant they really were."

Henson was not exceptional. It is probable that most slaves who managed to learn to read and write were determined to teach others. Eugene D. Genovese, in his landmark book, *Roll, Jordan, Roll: The World the Slaves Made* (1976), gives some examples:

"Elijah P. Marrs recalled an old plantation slave who had taught others after ten o'clock at

Family worship on a plantation in South Carolina

night. Sometimes a literate slave taught others with his master's permission, more often without it. An old black preacher in Georgia moaned on his dying bed that he had caused the death of many slaves by teaching them to read and write."

Slaves who worked in and around the homes of their owners were more likely to learn to read than those who were confined to the fields. House slaves had more opportunity to be exposed to books and newspapers. Some house slaves were treated as pets by members of the owner's family, and it was not unusual for children of the master to play with slave children and to teach them what they were learning. In many instances, it was probably white children who taught their black playmates how to read, in spite of their parents' prohibitions. There were many interracial friendships among young children before the white children were old enough to be turned away from that friendship by the customs and attitudes of society. In some cases, the slave child was the child of the master and some occupied a favored position. In other cases, masters or mistresses did the teaching, motivated variously by self-interest, conscience, religious belief, or a sense of democracy. An occasional master believed that it benefited him and his estate to have at least one or two literate slaves. An occasional mistress believed that slaves had souls and so should be able to read the Bible.

Some of the most telling anecdotes about slavery in the nineteenth century come from European visitors. One was Fanny Kemble, a famous English actress who arrived in the United States in 1832 for a triumphant two-year tour. In 1834, she married a wealthy young American, Pierce Butler, and began a new life. But her happiness soon turned to despair as she realized her husband expected complete obedience from her, and as she discovered the source of her husband's wealth. Butler was heir to the largest plantation in Georgia and master of seven hundred slaves. The marriage eventually ended in divorce and Kemble returned to the stage. She later wrote a book about her experiences as mistress of a Georgia plantation.

Kemble believed that it was an act against God to enslave other human beings, and she was skeptical of the ways slave owners rationalized slavery. She often encountered the prevailing wisdom that blacks were so stupid as to be incapable of instruction. Then, why, she wanted to know, was it necessary to have laws against teaching them? As she put it, "If they are incapable of profiting by instruction, I do not see the necessity for laws inflicting heavy penalties on those who offer it to them. . . .

We have no laws forbidding us to teach our dogs and horses as much as they can comprehend."

Kemble provides one of the recorded instances of a slave not wanting to learn. She met the slave son of another plantation owner. While the father was literate, the son was not. She suggested to the slave that he ask his father to teach him to read, but the young man answered hopelessly, "with a look and manner that went to my very heart. 'Missus, what for me learn to read? Me have no prospect.'"

Not just reading and writing but knowledge of mathematics was denied the slaves. A Dr. LeConte told a visiting Scotsman, the geologist Sir Charles Lyell, about the time his black carpenter excitedly sought him out to report he had discovered that each side of a hexagram equaled the radius of a circle drawn around it. LeConte replied that this was common knowledge. Stunned, the carpenter replied that had he been taught that, he could have made great use of it in his work.

Of the few blacks who managed to become literate against staggering odds, a substantial proportion probably taught themselves. Slave children who had to carry the books of white children to school would sit outside, listen, and try to keep up with the lessons. Here and there a slave would determinedly teach himself or herself.

Frederick Douglass asked Sophia Auld to teach him to read.

Such was the case with Frederick Douglass. Born a slave in 1817, as a young man he lived with the Auld family in Baltimore, Maryland. Sophia Auld read to him from the Bible, and he was fascinated by the relationship between the words coming from her mouth and the marks on the pages of the book. He had soon memorized some of the passages. Proud of her accomplishment, Mrs. Auld called on Frederick to show her husband what he had learned. Frederick dutifully "read" a passage from the Bible that he had memorized and was shocked, as was Sophia Auld, at Hugh Auld's reaction. The man launched into a tirade against teaching Frederick, or any other slave, to read. These angry words spilled from Auld's lips: "Learning would spoil the best nigger in the world. . . . If you teach that nigger . . . how to read the Bible, there will be no keeping him; it would forever unfit him for the duties of a slave; learning would do him no good, but probably, a great deal of harm — making him disconsolate and unhappy. . . . If you learn him how to read, he'll want to know how to write; and, this accomplished, he'll be running away with himself."

Years later, writing in his autobiography, Douglass described Auld's tirade as "oracular," by which he meant that the man accurately predicted his future. Although Sophia Auld's lessons stopped, Frederick persisted in his desire to learn to read. Down at the Baltimore docks, he watched men building ships and noticed that there were letters on the boards that indicated where the shipwrights were to place new parts. By the time he was eleven, he had recognized that letters could be joined to form words. Douglass matched the letters he had seen on the shipboards to those in the *Webster's Spelling Book* that belonged to the Aulds' son, Tommy. He secretly borrowed Tommy's school copybook and practiced writing those letters.

When Douglass was twelve, he saved up fifty cents and bought a copy of *The Columbian Orator* at a local bookstore. The book was a collection of great speeches from history. Douglass secretly read the words over and over. By the age of fourteen, he was teaching at the Sabbath school for black children at a local Methodist church.

In 1838, when he was twenty-one, Douglass did indeed, in Hugh Auld's words, "run away with himself," and he escaped to freedom. He went on to become one of the greatest orators in history, to publish antislavery newspapers, to write books, and to devote his life, his oratorical skills, and his writings to the antislavery cause.

Despite the prohibitions against slave literacy, perhaps 10 percent of the slaves were literate. The great African-American scholar W. E. B. Du Bois estimated that by 1860 about 5 percent of slaves had learned to read; but contemporary scholars place the estimate higher. Even this small percentage of literacy was accomplished against seemingly overwhelming odds.

4.

The New Nation — The North and Elsewhere

After independence from England, ideas of free public education gained in the North, and white public primary schools called common schools were established. But often, these schools were not open to free blacks, and certainly not to slaves. Even after slavery was abolished in most Northern states in the 1820s, these states offered few educational opportunities to blacks.

In some small communities in the North, black children were allowed to attend the local, predominantly white schools; but they were segregated. A black man named B. F. Grant described what it was like to go to school in York County, Pennsylvania:

"I will mention only a few things which the little Negro had to endure, simply because he was a Negro. He was not permitted to drink from the same bucket or cup as the white children. He was compelled to sit back in the corner from the fire no matter how cold the weather might be. There he must wait until the white children had recited. If the cold became *too* intense to endure, he must ask permission of the teacher, stand by the fire a few minutes to warm, and then return to the same cold corner. I have sat in an old log schoolhouse with no chinking between the logs until my heels were frostbitten and cracked open. Sometimes we had a poor white trashy skunk [of a teacher] that would sit in the schoolroom and call us 'niggers' or 'darkeys.' If the little Negro got his lesson at all, he got it; if not, it was all the same."

Most of the major cities did have some sort of formal educational opportunities for blacks, although they were separate schools and very uneven in quality. In 1827, John B. Russwurm, founder and editor of the New York City newspaper *Freedom's Journal,* the first African-American newspaper, published the following list of African Free Schools in the Northeast:

"Portland, Me. With a colored population of 900 provides one school under the care of a mistress.

"Boston, Mass. With a colored population of 2,000 provides three schools, two primary under the care of African female teachers, and a Grammar School under a master.

"Salem, Mass. With a colored population of 400, put a school into operation last year, but it closed after six months.

"New Haven, Conn. With a colored population of 800 provides two schools three months during the year.

"Providence, R.I. With a colored population of 1,500, and Hartford, Conn., with 500 provide none.

"Philadelphia. With a colored population of 15,000 provides three schools.

"New York. With a colored population of 15,000 provides two schools."

These schools were not public schools. Instead, they were sustained by philanthropy, primarily by white abolitionists and Quakers. Not until the 1830s did most larger cities begin to open public schools for blacks.

Among the earliest were the African Free Schools in New York, which operated from 1787 to 1860 and enrolled hundreds of students. One of their graduates, Ira Aldridge, went on to win international fame as a Shakespearean actor.

Other eminent products of the African Free Schools included John B. Russwurm, founder of *The Liberator* and one of the first two black graduates of American colleges, Henry Highland Garnet, James McCune Smith, and Alexander Crummell. At the African Free Schools, girls were taught separately from boys, and the subject matter they were taught differed. While boys studied

The actor Ira Aldridge graduated from one of the first African Free Schools in New York.

navigation and astronomy, girls were taught to sew and knit. The teachers at the African Free Schools were white. James McCune Smith, who attended one of the schools in the 1820s, recalled the dedication of his teacher, an Englishman by birth named Charles C. Andrews: "In spelling, penmanship, grammar, geography, and astronomy, he rightly boasted that his boys were equal, if not superior, to any like number of scholars in the city, and freely challenged competition at his Annual Examinations. In Natural Philosophy and Navigation, which were then new studies in a free school, he carried on classes as far as he was able, and then hired more competent teachers at his own expense. To stimulate his pupils, and bring out their varied talents, he instituted periodical fairs at which were exhibited the handiwork of the children.

"Mr. Andrews held that his pupils had as much capacity to acquire knowledge as any other children. It was thought by some, that he even regarded his black boys as a little smarter than whites. He taught his boys and girls to look upward; to believe themselves capable of accomplishing as much as any others could, and to regard the higher walks of life as within their reach."

In 1830, Andrews published *The History of the New-York African Free Schools,* in which he reproduced a valedictory speech delivered by a seven-year-old boy:

"This is my first appearance before you my friends, as a public speaker, and it becomes me to say but little. I am but seven years old, and I think I

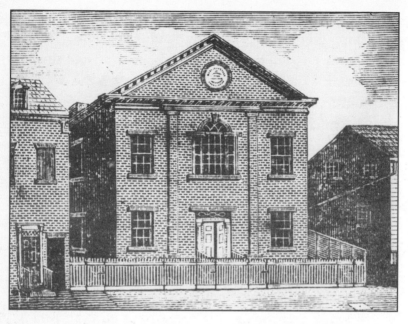

An engraving of the New York African Free School,
No. 2, made from a drawing by P. Reason, a pupil, aged thirteen years

have learned considerable since last examination. I
was then entirely ignorant of writing. I now present you with these humble specimens of my at-
tainments in that art. I was then also unacquainted
with the use of figures. I have since gone through
simple addition, subtraction, multiplication, and
division; I have some knowledge also of the com-
pound rules. I say not these things to magnify my
little self into something great, but to the credit of
the plan of instruction, and for the encouragement

of my schoolmates to improve the time while they have the advantage of an early education."

But for all his pride in his school, and all the promise of his students, Charles C. Andrews also recognized the reality of life for black students. In the same book, he reported the following question asked by a boy who was graduating from the school:

"Why should I strive hard, and acquire all the constituents of a man if the prevailing genius of the land admit me not as such? Pardon me if I feel insignificant and weak. Pardon me if I feel discouragement. Am I arrived at the end of my education, on the eve of commencing some pursuit by which to earn a comfortable subsistence? What are my prospects? Shall I be a mechanic? No one will employ me. White boys won't work with me. Drudgery and servitude are my prospective portion. Can you be surprised at my discouragement?"

In some areas, free blacks established their own schools. In Newport, Rhode Island, blacks organized an African Benevolent Society in 1808 whose purpose was "the establishment of a free school" for people of color. It remained in operation until 1842, when the first public school for black children opened in that city.

Elsewhere in Rhode Island, according to

a black shoemaker named William J. Brown (1814–1885), who grew up in Providence, "Some ladies opened a free school for colored youth," which he attended. In 1819, Brown related, the black community called a meeting for the purpose of building a meetinghouse, with a basement for a schoolroom. A local white businessman donated the land, and the house was finished in 1821. It then took the community some time to find a teacher, but at last they hired a white man named Mr. Ormsbee. Black parents had to pay tuition in the amount of $1.50 per quarter per student. Even so, the school soon had 125 students. Brown related in his autobiography:

"I attended the school at the opening. The scholars behaved pretty well. On the east side of the vestry there was a part that had never been dug out. It was partitioned off, leaving a dark hole twenty feet long having a door that opened in the vestry. Whenever any of the scholars misbehaved they were put in this hole. The children were very much afraid to be shut up in this place, for when they were digging the cellar they dug up a coffin and a man in it. They supposed it must have been some Indian that was buried there.

"Mr. Ormsbee was a very severe teacher. He used the cowhide very freely. After keeping the school for one year, his labors came to a close. For a year and a half the school was suspended, not being able to procure a teacher. Colored teachers were very rarely to be found, and it was difficult to procure a white teacher as it was considered disgraceful employment to be a teacher of colored children. . . . It was considered such a disgrace for white men to teach [in] colored schools that they would be greatly offended if the colored children bowed or spoke to them on the street."

Under such conditions, it is little wonder that even so-called educated blacks were poorly educated. David Walker was appalled by the sad state of black education in the North. Born in North Carolina in 1785, Walker had educated himself and moved to Boston in the 1820s. A voracious reader, Walker, while still in the South, had come to the conclusion that people of color were superior to whites in matters of character; that whites were unmerciful and driven by lust for material gain. Given the importance of learning to him, it was particularly tragic to Walker that Negroes had so few educational opportunities, and that even those available were sadly wanting. In 1829, Walker published an *Appeal to the Colored Citizens of the World,* in which he wrote:

"I have examined school-boys and young men of colour in different parts of the country, in the most simple parts of Murray's English Grammar, and not more than one in thirty was able to give a correct answer to my interrogations. If any one contradicts me, let him step out of his door into the streets of Boston, New-York, Philadelphia, or Baltimore. . . . I say, let him who disputes me, step out of his door into the streets of either of those four cities, and promiscuously collect one hundred schoolboys, or young men of colour, *who have been to school,* and who are considered by the coloured people to have received an excellent education . . ."

Walker, through his wide reading, knew of the achievements of blacks in the ancient world. His *Appeal* urged blacks throughout the world to unite against repression.

The *Appeal* created a storm — especially, of course, in the Southern states. Georgia and North Carolina passed laws to prevent "the circulation of seditous publications;" making it a crime for free Negroes to teach slaves to read. A group of white men in Georgia offered a reward of one thousand dollars for Walker dead, and ten times that amount for him alive. Friends urged Walker to flee to Canada, but he refused. There were rumors that his death in 1830 was a result of being poisoned; but those rumors were never proved.

More than a decade after Walker's death, blacks in Boston seemed to echo the charges of inferior education for blacks in his *Appeal*. In 1843, Boston's black community asked the school committee to close the public school for black children, charging that it was inferior. They signed petitions, held meetings, organized boycotts, and the next year sued in court to abolish separate schools for black children. It took more than ten years, but they finally won school integration in Boston.

African-American girls had even fewer opportunities than African-American boys. And in cases where a school admitted both boys and girls, the boys were clearly favored.

The Liberator, an antislavery journal published in Boston by the white abolitionist William Lloyd Garrison, reported wryly on July 9, 1831: "ADVANCING! At the Sabbath School Exhibition, held in Park-Street Church on the 4th of July, the colored boys were permitted to occupy pews one fourth of the way up the side aisle. The march of equality has certainly begun in Boston! The colored girls took their seats near the door, as usual."

In Canterbury, Connecticut, in 1832, a white woman named Prudence Crandall admitted a black student to her Female Boarding School. When the surrounding community objected, she refused to discharge the student. All her white students withdrew, whereupon Crandall in 1833 opened a boarding school for "Young Ladies and Little Misses of Color." She soon had twenty students from New York, Providence, Boston, and nearby Connecticut towns, each of whom paid twenty-five dollars per quarter in tuition. The townspeople of Canterbury reacted with fury. Neighbors refused to speak to Crandall; shopkeepers would not sell to her; local doctors would not accept the students as patients. Eggs and stones were thrown at the girls, and manure was dropped into the school's well. The Connecticut legislature passed a law that forbade out-of-state blacks from attending schools in Connecticut without the permission of local authorities. Crandall was then arrested for disobeying the law; but when her students were called to testify about where they lived, they refused. Crandall won her case on appeal; but an armed mob descended on the school, setting fire to it and smashing walls and windows. Crandall had no money to rebuild and was forced to close the school.

Even the children of distinguished black leaders were not spared the indignities of the public schools of Rochester, New York, where Frederick Douglass and his family lived. They were closed to black students until 1857. In September 1849, Douglass's daughter, Rosetta, who was eight or nine years old, applied to the private Seward Seminary in Rochester. The principal, a Miss Lucilia Tracy, admitted her to the school but would not allow her to be in the same room with the white students. When challenged by Frederick Douglass, the principal explained to Douglass that the trustees of the

Prudence Crandall admitted a black student to her Female Boarding School and was arrested for disobeying the law.

school were opposed to having a black student. After Douglass threatened to withdraw his daughter from the school, the principal decided to ask each student how she felt about the presence of the Douglass girl. All the students were eager to welcome her. But then Miss Tracy asked the girls to put the issue to their parents. One father objected, and Douglass's daughter had to leave the school. In the March 30, 1849, issue of his newspaper, *The North Star*, Douglass wrote an open letter to that parent, who just happened to be H. B. Warner, editor of the *Rochester Courier*. In the letter, Douglass asked, "I should like to know how much better you are than me, and how much better your children than mine? We differ in color, it is true, but who is to decide which color is most pleasing to God, or most honorable among men?"

Rosetta Douglass was then tutored privately by a white woman, after which she went to Oberlin College for a year in the preparatory department. Founded by abolitionists, Oberlin was the first coeducational, interracial college in the country. Many of the black students were from the South, the children of slave mothers whose white fathers wanted to educate them.

Charlotte Forten, granddaughter of the respected black Philadelphia leader James Forten, attended an integrated school in Salem, Massachusetts, although she had to live with friends rather than at the school. She wrote in her journal about her experiences:

"Wednesday, September 12, 1855. Today school commenced. I wonder that every colored person is not a misanthrope. Surely we have everything to make us hate mankind. I have met girls in the schoolroom. They have been thoroughly kind and cordial to me. Perhaps the next day met them in the street — they feared to recognize me. Others give the most distant recognition possible. I, of course, acknowledge no such recognitions, and they soon cease entirely. These are but trifles, certainly, to the great public wrongs which we as a people are obliged to endure. But to those who experience them, these apparent trifles are most wearing and discouraging. Even to a child's mind, they reveal volumes of deceit and heartlessness, and early teach a lesson of suspicion and distrust. Oh! it is hard to go through life meeting contempt with contempt, hatred with hatred, fearing, with too good reason, to love and trust hardly anyone whose skin is white."

All the schools for blacks were grammar schools. There were no high schools for blacks, and certainly no colleges.

The first American-born black to receive a thorough formal education was John Chavis. Born

Charlotte Forten, who attended an integrated school in Massachusetts, later became a teacher and opened a school for the children of ex-slaves.

and raised in North Carolina, he attended Princeton University in Princeton, New Jersey, although he did not officially graduate. For thirty years he taught in a school in Wake County, North

Carolina. In a rare departure from prevailing custom, which ordinarily barred blacks from teaching whites, he taught white boys during the day and black boys at night (girls were not allowed to be students at the school). In 1831, the state of North Carolina passed laws prohibiting the education of Negroes, and Chavis was forced to leave his position.

Except in such rare cases, black men who wished a formal education were forced to go abroad. Alexander Crummell studied at Queen's College in Cambridge, England. James McCune Smith went to Glasgow University in Scotland for his medical degree. The majority of colleges for whites refused to admit blacks until a few began to do so in the middle 1820s, when slavery was abolished in the North. Edward Jones and John Russwurm, who graduated in 1826 from Amherst College in Massachusetts and Bowdoin College in Maine, respectively, were the first black graduates of American colleges. Dartmouth College in Hanover, New Hampshire, began accepting black men in 1824; Wesleyan University in Middletown, Connecticut, in 1832; and Oberlin College in Oberlin, Ohio did so in 1833.

In 1831, the Convention of the People of Color, meeting in Philadelphia, resolved to start what was called a "manual labor college" where blacks could learn trades as well as academic subjects. Among those spearheading the effort were James Forten and Robert Douglass, son of Frederick Douglass. The plan was to build the seminary in New Haven, Connecticut. But when word reached New Haven, the citizens held a town meeting and voted to "resist the establishment of the proposed College in this place, by every lawful means." The college was never built. Later attempts to found a college for black students also failed.

Not until much later were black women accepted at American colleges. Born a slave in Washington, D.C., a daugher of her master, Fanny Jackson was purchased by her aunt and then sent to live with another aunt in Massachusetts. This aunt sent her out to work as a domestic, and Jackson was pleased that her employer allowed her to attend school when she was not needed at work. "But I could not go on wash day, nor ironing day, nor cleaning day, and this interfered with my progress," she later wrote. Jackson was determined to get an education, explaining, "It was in me to get an education and to teach my people. The idea was deep in my soul." She managed to graduate from Rhode Island Normal School, a training school for teachers, and then from Oberlin College with a bachelor of arts degree in 1865. She then went to work at the Institute for Colored Youth in Philadelphia, rose to the position of principal in 1869, and remained there until her retirement in 1902.

States in the Midwest were settled later than those in the East, and therefore established public institutions later. In Illinois in 1849, the state legislature wrote a new constitution that provided for state-supported public schools. It also voted to exclude black children. While the issue was being debated, a free man of color named Frank, who had been born a slave in South Carolina in 1777 and who had traveled to western Illinois and set up his own town, New Philadelphia, began to arrange for the construction of the Free Will Baptist Seminary. In the meantime, Free Frank, as he was known, rented an existing public schoolhouse for use by his grandchildren and the other resident black children.

The far West was still so sparsely populated in the mid-nineteenth century that there were few if any schools for black children. In Sacramento, California, a Reverend Jeremiah Sanderson opened a school in 1854 for what he judged to be the approximately thirty black children who lived there and for whom the authorities had provided no school. Finally, in 1856, the Sacramento Board of Education opened a school for black children.

In San Francisco, in 1862, eleven black parents wrote a letter of protest to *The Pacific Appeal,* complaining about the conditions in which fifty children were forced to try to learn, and stating, "There are now upwards of three hundred colored children in this city. To accommodate them we need another, better and larger place. We need a school of a higher grade. We need additional teachers. We feel the same anxiety touching the future of our children that you feel for yours."

Whatever the region, education for blacks was a scattershot affair until the post-Civil War period, when the expanded power of the federal government, and new ideas of states' responsibilities to their citizens would alter the nature of education in the nation for everyone.

5.

War and Reconstruction

The question of slavery had plagued the United States since its founding. It had forced compromises in the writing of the United States Constitution and continued to be a stumbling block for the next three quarters of a century. Every time a new state sought admission to the Union, there were arguments about whether it should be slave or free. Southern congressmen would not vote to admit a free state unless a slave state was also admitted, thereby maintaining a balance. By the 1850s, the struggle between free and slave states threatened to split the nation in two; and in 1860, it did. In December 1860, following the election of Republican Abraham Lincoln to the presidency, South Carolina seceded from the Union, soon followed by Alabama, Florida, Georgia, Louisiana, Mississippi, and Texas. The secessionist states formed a new union called the Confederate States of America; and on April 14, 1861, with the Confederate attack on the federal Fort Sumter in South Carolina, the Civil War began.

Four long and bloody years later, the South lay

Abraham Lincoln issued the Emancipation Proclamation, freeing all slaves in the Confederate States.

vanquished and the era of slavery in the United States was over. After the war, Congress took steps to ensure that slavery would never return and that the former slaves would be guaranteed equal rights of citizenship by law. These steps took the form of three amendments to the United States Constitution, the Thirteenth, Fourteenth, and Fifteenth.

The Thirteenth Amendment (1865) outlawed slavery, stating, "Neither slavery nor involuntary servitude . . . shall exist within the United States, or any place subject to its jurisdiction."

The Fourteenth Amendment (1868) guaranteed citizenship to the former slaves. It defined a citizen of the United States as anyone born or naturalized in the United States and stated, "No State shall make or enforce any law which shall abridge the privileges or immunities of citizens of the United States; nor shall any State deprive any person of life, liberty, or property, without due process of law; nor deny to any person within its jurisdiction the equal protection of the laws."

The Fifteenth Amendment (1870) granted the right to vote to blacks, stating, "The right of citizens of the United States to vote shall not be denied or abridged by the United States or by any State on account of race, color, or previous condition of servitude."

All three amendments were ratified during the post-Civil War period of rebuilding in the war-ravaged South that was called Reconstruction. During Reconstruction, federal troops occupied the former Confederate states, which were ordered to draft new constitutions ensuring liberty for the former slaves. The states were expected to ratify the new amendments to the Constitution as a condition for readmittance to the Union. President Lincoln had believed that the South had been punished enough and planned to return to the losing side in the war as many rights as possible as soon as possible. But Lincoln did not live to carry out his plans for rebuilding the South. An embittered Southerner named John Wilkes Booth assassinated the president. Under Lincoln's vice president, Andrew Johnson, who succeeded him in office, Congress instituted a far harsher and more repressive Reconstruction aimed at punishing the former Confederate states.

Under what was called Radical Reconstruction, most former Confederates and Confederate sympathizers were denied the right to vote, leaving the power to draft the new state constitutions in the hands of Northerners who went south and Southern Republicans, or supporters of the majority party in Congress. The Northerners were called carpetbaggers because hand luggage in those days was often made of carpet material. The white Republican Southerners were called scalawags, a term usually reserved for an animal of little value. In a few areas, blacks, some of the former slaves, also participated in the Reconstruction governments; and in some states, such as South Carolina, they were actually in the majority in the Reconstruction legislatures. But in general, blacks were unable to participate because they were illiterate.

There were many ways in which the freedmen, as the former slaves were called, were not ready for freedom. They had no land and no property. Even the clothes on their backs were the property of their former owners. They had few skills, except those that made them good workers for white owners. They were not accustomed to independence and had few tools for asserting it. But the severest problem was their lack of education.

To help the slaves adjust to freedom and become self-sufficient, Congress authorized creation of the Freedmen's Bureau, whose agents established courts, hospitals, charitable institutions, and labor regulations to assist the former slaves. These institutions and regulations were supposed to be temporary, until local authorities recognized blacks as equals and the forces of the free market came to govern economic relations. Bureau officials believed that blacks would benefit more by recognition as equal citizens than from being treated as a special class permanently dependent upon federal assistance and protection.

The one bureau activity that was not designed to be temporary was the creation of a system of education for the freedmen. The Freedmen's Bureau considered education the foundation for black equality; and local agents spent a significant portion of their time encouraging and overseeing schools. Education probably represents the agency's greatest success in the postwar South.

Before the war, every Southern state except Tennessee had prohibited the instruction of slaves. After the war, former slaves released their pent-up thirst for education. White contemporaries were astonished at the freedmen's desire for learning. In Mississippi, a Freedmen's Bureau agent reported in 1865 that when he informed a gathering of three thousand freedmen that they "were to have the advantages of schools and education, their joy knew no bounds. They fairly jumped and shouted in gladness."

The desire for learning led black parents to migrate to towns and cities; and plantation workers made the establishment of a schoolhouse "an absolute condition" of signing labor contracts. (One 1867 Louisiana contract specified that the planter pay a 5 percent tax to support black education.) Adults as well as children thronged to schools established during and after the Civil War. A Northern teacher in Florida reported how one sixty-year-old woman "just beginning to spell, seems as if she could not think of any thing but her book, says she spells her lesson all evening, then she dreams about it, and wakes up thinking about it."

For many adults, a craving to read "the word of God" was the impetus for learning. One elderly freedman sitting beside his grandchild in a Mobile, Alabama, school explained to a Northern reporter that "he wouldn't trouble the lady much, but he must learn to read the Bible and the Testament." Others recognized education as indispensable for economic advancement. "I gets almost discouraged, but I dos want to learn to cipher so I can do business," an elderly Mississippi pupil told his teacher.

Northern benevolent societies and, after 1868, state governments joined the Freedmen's Bureau to fund black education during Reconstruction. But the initiative often lay with blacks themselves. Even before the war was over, blacks had started establishing schools in the South. When members of the Gideons, a Bible society, arrived in the Sea Islands off South Carolina in 1862, they reported finding "two schools already in operation, one of

A primary school for freedmen in Vicksburg, Mississippi

them taught by a black cabinetmaker who for years had conducted secret night classes for slaves."

In other rural areas, Freedmen's Bureau officials repeatedly expressed surprise at discovering classes organized by blacks meeting in churches, basements, or private homes. Children taught their parents at home. A bureau officer described what were called wayside schools: "A negro riding on a loaded wagon, or sitting on a hack waiting for a train, or by the cabin door, is often seen, book in hand, delving after the rudiments of knowledge. A group on the platform of a depot, after carefully conning an old spelling book, resolves itself into a class."

After the war, blacks in cities acted without delay to set up schools, in some places holding classes temporarily in abandoned warehouses and even slave markets. Less than a month after Union troops occupied Richmond, Virginia, in April 1865, over one thousand black children and seventy-five adults attended schools established by Richmond's black churches and the American Missionary Society.

Throughout the South, blacks in 1865 and 1866 formed societies and raised money among themselves to purchase land, build schoolhouses, and pay teachers' salaries. It was a burden for impoverished communities to fund schools. As one Northern educator remarked, "Contemporaries could not but note the contrast between white families seemingly indifferent to education and blacks who 'toil and strive, labour and endure in order that their children may have a schooling.'" He added, "It is not significant that after the lapse of one hundred and forty-four years since the settlement [of Beaufort, North Carolina], the Freedmen are building the first public school-house ever erected here."

By 1870, blacks had spent over $1 million of their own money on education. But eventually they had to turn elsewhere for help — to the Freedmen's Bureau and missionary societies.

The Freedmen's Bureau itself had limited resources for education. Its energies in that area were directed at coordinating the activities of Northern societies committed to black education. By 1869, nearly 3,000 schools, serving over 150,000 pupils, reported to the bureau. Plagued by financial difficulties and inadequate facilities, and more successful in reaching blacks in towns and cities than in rural areas, the bureau schools nevertheless helped lay the foundation for Southern public education.

In some states, local whites, some with deeply racist attitudes, staffed the freedmen's schools; but most of the teachers were middle-class white Northern women, the majority from New England, sent south by Northern aid societies such as the American Missionary Society, the Friends Association of Philadelphia and New York, the New England Freedmen's Aid Society, and others. The American Missionary Society was the largest of these groups, supporting more than 5,000 teachers in the South between 1861 and 1876. They opened schools wherever they could find space — in army barracks, church basements, even slave pens. They taught children by day and adults at night. They followed the Union armies, carrying primers and Bibles to liberated areas. When the war ended, they also moved into other areas of the South.

Of these white Northern missionary teachers, most were single and childless. Almost all were in their twenties, with an above-average education. Most had taught before going south. Most were very committed to their responsibilities, and likened their service to that of Northern male soldiers in the war. Many faced battles of their own in the South, including local prejudice, low pay, and poor living conditions. Conditions were much worse for the African-American teachers, who in several cases had to room with domestics.

Scores of the teachers who taught in the South during and after the Civil War were black. Mary S. Peake was the first black teacher to be supported by a Northern society. Born free in Virginia and educated in a private school in Washington, D.C., she had taught slaves and free blacks before the war. In September 1861, a month after Hampton, Virginia, had been evacuated by Confederate forces, she arrived in the town under the auspices of the American Missionary Society. There, she taught without pay, first in a church and then, after it was burned, elsewhere. She contracted tuberculosis but continued to teach from her bedside until her death in February 1862 at the age of thirty-nine, leaving a husband and a child. From that small school developed Hampton Institute, one of the most distinguished colleges for blacks.

Many of the early black teachers were not as well educated as Mary Peake. Yet, they wanted to help the freedmen. One wrote to the Freedmen's Bureau education officials: "I have no education only what I gave myself by chance so I ask you to excuse my unqualified address." Another wrote, "I never had the chance of goen to school for I was a slave until freedom. . . . I am the only teacher because we can not doe better now."

With assistance from the Freedmen's Bureau, Northern societies also founded and staffed the first black colleges in the South, including Berea, Fisk, Hampton, and Tougaloo, all initially designed to train black teachers. By 1869, among the approximately three thousand freedmen's teachers in the South, blacks for the first time outnumbered whites. They did much more than teach. They functioned as community leaders. They assisted freedmen in contract disputes, engaged in church work, and drafted petitions to the Freedmen's Bureau, state officials, and Congress. At least seventy black teachers served in state legislatures during Reconstruction, the majority of them having been free before the Civil War.

The Reconstruction governments were unique in several ways, not the least of which was that African Americans served in them. They were also enlightened in their attempts to pass legislation that would benefit all, both blacks and whites. Racist caricatures of the time portrayed the Reconstruction legislatures as bunches of illiterate, corrupt monkeys. Indeed, some were illiterate and some were corrupt. But most had a vision of a democratic society in which all could enjoy opportunity.

Despite traditions of local autonomy that resisted state-run and -controlled institutions such as public school systems, and despite the financial burdens, a public school system gradually took shape in the Reconstruction South. Whites in-

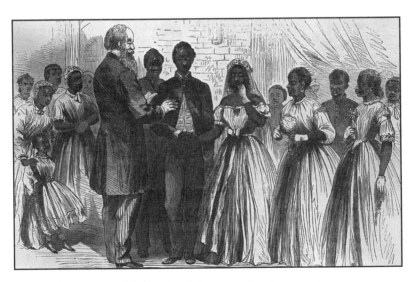

Chaplain Warren of the Freedmen's Bureau performing a marriage ceremony

creasingly took advantage of the new educational opportunities. Texas had 1,500 schools by 1872, with the majority of the children enrolled. By 1875, in Mississippi, Florida, and South Carolina, about half the children of both races attended. Schooling continued to be far more available in cities and towns. By 1880, the black population, which remained predominantly rural, also remained 70 percent illiterate. Nonetheless, for the first time in Southern history, the principle of state responsibility for public education was established.

6.

The Doctrine of "Separate But Equal"

By 1876, both the South and the North were tired of the disruptions of Radical Reconstruction and eager to reunite the nation so it could pursue economic growth. Soon after his election as president, Rutherford B. Hayes, a Republican, declared Reconstruction ended. Federal troops left the South, the Freedmen's Bureau ceased operations, and black Southerners were left to fend for themselves. It took some years, but racist Southerners eventually dismantled most of the democratic achievements of the Reconstruction period.

Mississippi was the first state to take the vote away from blacks. The main purpose of its new state constitution in 1890 was to disenfranchise blacks. Because the Fifteenth Amendment forbade discrimination on the basis of "race, color, or previous condition of servitude," the framers of the new Mississippi constitution devised other ways to deny blacks the vote. They instituted such barriers as a requirement that only those who owned property worth at least $300 to $500 could vote; a "literacy test," which most blacks could not pass because they had been denied an education; and a poll tax to be paid for the right to register to vote. These requirements effectively disenfranchised the great majority of black voters. When the United States Supreme Court in 1898 upheld what was called the Mississippi Plan, other Southern states soon followed suit; and by 1910 all had established variations of the plan.

But legal disenfranchisement was not enough for white supremacists in the South. Hand in hand with disenfranchisement came a multiplication of

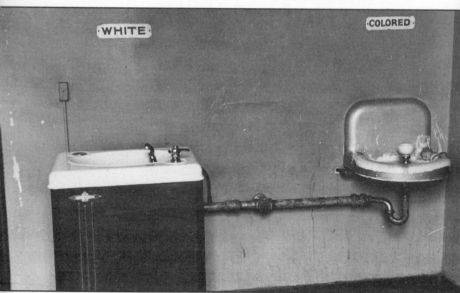

Segregated water fountains in North Carolina

so-called Jim Crow laws. Named after a comic stage character played by a white man in blackface, but based on an old black man who did a funny dance, Jim Crow laws introduced segregation into every walk of life. In 1881, Tennessee segregated black passengers on railway cars; Florida followed in 1887. Louisiana passed a similar law in 1890, creating separate railroad cars for whites and blacks.

In education, the public school systems that had begun in Reconstruction were cut back or dismantled; by the 1880s less than a third of the black children of the South received free schooling. By 1889–1890, only 32.8 percent of school-age blacks in the South were enrolled in public schools.

Booker T. Washington (1856–1915) could see the handwriting on the wall. The South blamed blacks for the Civil War and the vanquishment of the South; the North was tired of all the upheaval and no friend to the Negro either. African Americans could not expect much sympathy or help. It was best to bow to prevailing attitudes.

Booker T. Washington was the founder, in 1881, of Tuskegee Institute in Alabama, which functioned as a school for the training of black teachers. With a grant of $2,000 a year from the Alabama State Legislature, Washington managed to build the school into a respected institution that was well funded by Northern philanthropists. One reason why he was able to attract this money was that he did not teach academic subjects. Rather, he taught blacks trades, to work with their hands, to learn to be farmers and carpenters. Washington firmly believed in the theory that economics was the way to equality; that if blacks could, through work and thrift, build an economic power base of their own, social equality would follow. Until that time, he believed, there was no point in fighting prejudice.

Washington's views found a sympathetic audience among Southern businessmen who wished to renew commercial ties with the North and help the South move from its dependence on agriculture. It was Washington's well-known views that led to his invitation to speak at the 1895 Cotton States and International Exposition in Atlanta, Georgia, to which exhibitors from all the then forty-four states and many foreign countries had been invited. Washington did not disappoint his hosts. He delivered a ringing speech that unwittingly would set the tone for what was to come:

"Ignorant and inexperienced, it is not strange that in the first years of our new life we began at the top instead of at the bottom; that a seat in Congress or the State Legislature was more sought than real estate or industrial skill; that the political convention or stump speaking had more attraction than starting a dairy farm or truck garden."

He went on to say, "No race can prosper till it learns that there is as much dignity in tilling a field as in writing a poem. It is at the bottom of life we must begin and not at the top . . ."

The high point of Washington's speech came when he raised his hand above his head, fingers stretched wide apart. "In all things that are purely social we can be as separate as the fingers," he said, "yet as one hand in all things essential to mutual progress."

To thundering applause and cheers, Booker T. Washington established himself as a major spokesman for what is called the "accommodationist" point of view.

His speech was applauded not only by Southerners but also by Northerners — at least by whites in both regions. Not a few blacks also believed that the path he advocated was the best, although it was a painful admission. James Creelman, a reporter for the *New York World*, wrote that at the end of the speech, "Most of the Negroes in the audience were crying, perhaps without knowing why." They were crying over dashed hopes that the promise of the Emancipation Proclamation, the Northern victory in the Civil War, and the years of Reconstruction had all held out in their time. Some were also crying in the renewed hope that perhaps Washington had discovered the key to their finally being acknowledged as human beings in American society. And some were also crying because, in their eyes, Washington's speech and the powerful positive reaction to it were admissions of defeat — that African Americans would never be recognized as equal human beings.

John Hope was in the audience to hear Booker T. Washington's speech. He had been offered a job at Tuskegee and had turned it down. Later, he would become president of Atlanta University. Several months after Washington's speech, he wrote a reply. In it, he said:

"If we are not striving for equality, in heaven's name for what are we living? I regard it as cowardly and dishonest for any of our colored men to tell white people or colored people that we are not struggling for equality.... Let us not fool ourselves nor be fooled by others. If we cannot do what other freemen do, then we are not free. Yes, my friends, I want equality. Nothing less ...

Booker T. Washington (seated front row, left) founded the Tuskegee Institute.

"Rise Brothers! . . . Never say, 'Let well enough alone.' . . . Be discontented. Be dissatisfied. . . . Let your discontent break mountain-high against the wall of prejudice and swamp it. . . . Then we shall not have to plead for justice nor on bended knee crave mercy; for we shall be men . . ."

But there was little stimulus for Southern blacks to rise. Their Northern white friends had deserted them. They had few Southern white friends. They felt powerless to affect their conditions, knowing that to protest was to invite furious retribution. Lynchings, or murders of blacks for real or perceived slights, had reached epidemic proportions. The nation, and history, were against them. The very federal government that had sought to support them during Reconstruction was in the hands of other men now, men who believed it was time to get on with the business of national economic growth and to return to the states the rights they had once enjoyed.

Booker T. Washington's image of the hand with spread fingers, and his words about blacks and whites being separate in all things social, proved to be prophetic. Just one year after he made that speech the United States Supreme Court made "separate but equal" the law of the land.

The Court's decision was handed down in the case of *Plessy* v. *Ferguson,* which concerned the issue of segregated transportation. After the state of Louisiana had instituted a law separating the races in railway cars in 1890, a mulatto named Homer

The Doctrine of "Separate But Equal"

Plessy entered a car marked FOR WHITES ONLY and refused the conductor's order to move. He was arrested and later sued the state of Louisiana for violating his rights. His lawyers argued that being forbidden to ride in the same railroad car as whites marked him as inferior, or less of a man, than white passengers. Lawyers for the state argued in return that separate cars for Negroes were not a mark of inferiority, as long as the cars were "equal."

At issue was the meaning of the Fourteenth Amendment to the Constitution, passed in 1868. It stated, "No State shall make or enforce any law which shall abridge the privileges or immunities of citizens of the United States; nor shall any State deprive any person of life, liberty, or property, without due process of law; nor deny to any person within its jurisdiction the equal protection of the laws."

The Supreme Court acknowledged that the Fourteenth Amendment was intended to make the two races "equal" under the law. However, it went on to say, "If one race be inferior to the other socially, the Constitution of the United States cannot put them on the same plane. The distinction between the two races . . . founded on the color of the two races, must always exist so long as white men are distinct from the other color."

Only one justice refused to go along with the majority in the Court's ruling. Justice John Marshall Harlan, a former slaveholder from Kentucky, had fought on the Union side during the Civil War. He wrote in his dissenting opinion, "Our Constitution is color-blind, and neither knows nor tolerates classes among citizens. . . . The law regards man as man, and takes no account of his surroundings or of his color."

But Harlan's was a voice in the wilderness. The largely Southern, pro-segregation Court was determined to "put Negroes in their place" by law.

The Court did not define just what was meant by equal, and Southern states never intended even to try to provide equal accommodations. What they wanted was complete segregation in all areas of life and to punish the people whom they blamed for the Civil War and the end of slavery by forcing them to live in degrading and insulting conditions. The Supreme Court's ruling in *Plessy* v. *Ferguson* in 1896 gave a legal approval to what they were doing anyway, and unleashed a tidal wave of new segregation laws in the South.

By the early 1900s, ten Southern states had laws segregating blacks on streetcars. Simultaneously, laws were introduced segregating, or barring blacks entirely, at sporting events, at movie theaters, in public parks, in restaurants, and at just about every other public facility. Prisons, orphanages, and asylums for the mentally ill were no exception.

The tide of segregation was so strong that some localities passed petty ordinances, such as the one in Birmingham, Alabama, that forbade blacks and whites from playing checkers together, and the one in South Carolina that barred the two races from looking out the same cotton mill window.

In education, laws that echoed those existing in the time of slavery were instituted in many localities, forbidding white teachers from teaching black children. Florida passed a statute that not only required separate Negro and white textbooks but also decreed that they be stored separately in warehouses.

Following these laws were the customs of segregation, all aimed at making blacks feel subhuman. White store clerks refused to accept money from, or to put change into, the hands of blacks. Rather, the money was to be placed on the counter. When a white and a black approached each other on the same sidewalk or the same side of the street, the black had to step aside. White laundry establishments advertised that they only did whites' laundry. The degradation of blacks went on and on and on.

As the years passed, many more blacks began to question Booker T. Washington's "Atlanta Compromise," arguing that it was no compromise at all, but simply an acquiesence to degradation. Hard work and thrift had not uplifted the Negro. Instead, blacks had been relegated to the lowest jobs in the very industries that were supposed to lift up the South and the nation as a whole — janitors in the new factories, diggers in the coal mines, track builders and repairers of the railroads. African-American women continued to be the caretakers of white children, the cleaners of white houses, the laundresses of whites' soiled clothing. In the meantime, agriculture, the former mainstay of the Southern economy, had become increasingly mechanized, making large numbers of black agricultural workers less necessary.

By the turn of the century, Northern-born young black intellectuals had begun to speak out against segregation. William Monroe Trotter founded the *Boston Guardian* in 1901 and used the paper's editorial pages to demand freedom for the Negro. He called Booker T. Washington a "traitor to his race." William Edward Burghardt Du Bois had roomed with Trotter at Harvard and received his Ph.D. from Harvard University in the year

W. E. B. Du Bois, one of the founders of the National Association for the Advancement of Colored People

Booker T. Washington had given his famous speech at the Atlanta Exposition. In 1903, Du Bois published a collection of essays, *The Souls of Black Folk*. One essay attacked Booker T. Washington for depending on the goodwill of white people. Du Bois wrote that Washington had, in effect, asked black people to give up their essential rights. Du Bois urged African-Americans to demand these rights, especially three: 1) the right to vote; 2) civic equality; and 3) the education of youth according to ability. Du Bois ended by urging, "By every civilized and peaceful method we must strive for the rights which the world accords to men, clinging unwaveringly to those great words (from the Declaration of Independence) . . . : 'We hold these truths to be self-evident; that all men are created equal, that they are endowed by their Creator with certain unalienable rights, that among these are life, liberty and the pursuit of happiness.'"

By the end of his life, Booker T. Washington himself had begun to question the wisdom of his compromise. In the twenty years since his Atlanta Exposition speech, he had enjoyed the position of the most powerful and influential black man in America. He had advised business leaders and politicians and scholars. He had counseled presidents. He had been the first Negro to have dinner with a president at the White House.

But even he had not been allowed to be a man. Southern newspapers had criticized his dining at the White House. While traveling in the South, he had been subjected to the indignities of segregation. After Washington's death in 1915, *The New Republic* magazine published an essay he had written in which he admitted what segregation had meant for the Negro:

"Inferior accommodations in return for the taxes he pays . . . that the sewerage in his part of the city will be inferior; that the streets and sidewalks will be neglected; that the street lighting will be poor; that his section of the city will not be kept in order by the police and other authorities, and that . . . it will be difficult for him to rear his family in decency."

Many average Southern blacks had long since come to the same conclusions; and since they had no hope of making life better in the South, they began to leave. W. E. B. Du Bois had urged black Southerners to go north after antiblack riots in Atlanta, Georgia, in 1906: "We might as well face the facts squarely; if there is any colored man in the South who wishes to have his children educated and who wishes to be in close touch with civilization and who has any ghost of a chance of making a living in the North it is his business to get out of the South as soon as possible. . . . The only effective protest that the Negroes . . . can make against lynching and disfranchisement is through leaving the devilish country where these things take place."

The advent of World War I gave many Southern blacks that "ghost of a chance of making it."

When World War I broke out in Europe in 1914, scores of recent European immigrants returned to their homelands to fight. At the same time, the United States passed laws restricting foreign immigration. These combined events opened up new employment opportunities for blacks in Northern urban centers, where the nation's chief industries were located. These new job opportunities in the North, combined with the degrading conditions for blacks in the South, helped spur an unprecedented migration of Southern blacks to the North.

Between 1915 and 1918, hundreds of thousands of African Americans headed to such Midwestern cities as Chicago, Cleveland, and Detroit, and to such Eastern cities as New York, Philadelphia, and Boston. Whatever the city, the migration caused great social upheaval. Many Southern blacks had difficulty adjusting to urban life. The Urban League, an interracial organization, was formed in 1910 for the express purpose of helping the recent arrivals. Many Northern whites hated and feared the newcomers. Antiblack feelings ran high and resulted in greater discrimination in the North as well as greater antiblack violence. In many areas, blacks were being beaten, lynched, and murdered. In East St. Louis, Illinois, in early July 1917, whites rioted against blacks, murdering hundreds, beating thousands more, and destroying thousands of homes.

Life in the North, was "no piece of cake," according to Sadie and Bessie Delany, who published a joint memoir in 1993, when they were 103 and 101, respectively. But it was still better than Raleigh, North Carolina, where they had been born and raised. As young women, both were determined to get advanced degrees and to be professionals, and that meant going to the North to school. One of their brothers had settled in New York City, and they went there.

Sadie wanted to be a teacher, and she enrolled at Pratt Institute for a two-year course. There had been no chemistry labs at St. Augustine's School in Raleigh, which she had attended, so she was weak in that area. "That was a problem for a lot of col-

*Hillary Rodham Clinton visiting with Dr. Bessie Delany (left)
and Sadie Delany (right).*

ored students," she said. "Often, our early training
was not as good as the white students' because colored schools had no money. Then, you had to
struggle to keep up if you got into a white college,
and white people would label you 'dumb.'"

Both sisters found that they had to suffer from
whites' stereotypes of blacks: that they were lazy
and dishonest. At Pratt, Sadie received a C in
chemistry even though she had gotten an A on the
final exam. When she asked her instructor why, he
said it was because she had not participated in
class. Being shy and lacking confidence, Sadie had
been reluctant to raise her hand for fear of giving a

wrong answer; but the instructor said she was lazy. She protested the grade, and in a compromise, received a B.

In her final semester, Sadie had to borrow twenty-five dollars from the school. She paid it back as fast as she could. Several years later, she received a letter from the school demanding repayment. She was able to prove that she had indeed repaid the loan, but was certain that the insulting tone of the letter was due to her race. "When you're colored, people think you're dishonest," she said.

After Pratt, Sadie enrolled at Columbia University to complete her teaching degree. When it came time for her to do practice-teaching, she was assigned to a settlement house rather than to a public school classroom. She finally won the right to practice-teach in the same school system as her white classmates.

Bessie Delany was determined to become a dentist, and she enrolled at dental school at Columbia University in the fall of 1919. Out of a class of 170, there were six black men. There were also eleven women, of which she was the only black.

One of her experiences with racism at the school occurred when she received a failing grade for her work in a course. As an experiment, one of her white female classmates handed in the same work, and the instructor passed her. "That was the kind of thing that could make you crazy, as a Negro," said Bessie Delany. "It's no wonder some of us have stopped trying altogether. But as my Papa used to say, 'Don't ever give up. Remember, they can segregate you, but they can't control your mind. Your mind's still yours.'"

Bessie was accused of stealing while at Columbia. After the students' dental equipment started disappearing, the police were called, and all the women students were summoned to the women's locker area. The police asked Bessie to open her locker, and they searched it. While the locker was open, the actual thief tossed a piece of dental equipment into it. Fortunately, Bessie saw her, and the police arrested the young woman. If she had not seen the thief's action, Bessie Delany reported years later, she would have been falsely arrested. "And she [the culprit] knew she'd have gotten away with it because it would be easy for everyone to believe that this little darkey was a thief. Now, that just kills me."

Even on graduation day, June 6, 1923, Delany ran into prejudice at Columbia. "The class selected me as the marshall, and I thought it was an honor.

And then I found out — I heard them talking — it was because no one wanted to march beside me in front of their parents. It was a way to get rid of me."

But for all the pain and humiliation African Americans experienced in the North, it was nothing compared to life in the South, where segregation was the law.

7.

Groundwork

Black people continued to see education as the most important way to lift themselves out of poverty and despair. But in the segregated South they had little hope of getting a quality education. Between September 1926 and July 1928, *Crisis*, the official publication of the NAACP, ran a series of articles based on the results of studies it had conducted on school financing in several Southern states. These studies, paid for by a grant from the Garland Fund, revealed the huge disparity between state expenditures for white and black students. The report on Georgia, for example, revealed an average per pupil expenditure of $36.29 for whites and $4.59 for blacks, an eight-to-one ratio. Average teacher salaries were $97.88 per month for whites and $49.41 for blacks. In Mississippi, the ratio of expenditures on white versus black students was five to one. In South Carolina, there were similar disparities in per student spending and teacher salaries; and the class size for black students in South Carolina was, on average, twice that of white students.

In North Carolina, the disparities were much smaller; the ratio of per pupil spending for whites was only two times that for blacks. The average class size in the white schools was 26.3, as compared to 30.5 pupils in black schools. White teachers' salaries averaged $98.20 per month, while those for blacks averaged $66.53. But these statistics were still alarming, considering how important education was to young lives.

W. E. B. Du Bois, one of the founders of the NAACP in 1909, was the editor of *Crisis*. In an editorial written after the series of articles ended, he wrote, "The next step for the National Association for the Advancement of Colored People is a forward movement all along the line to secure justice for Negro children in the schools of the nation. . . . In open defiance of the Constitution . . . and of their own state laws, the funds dedicated to education . . . are systematically spent so as to discriminate against colored children and keep them in ignorance. . . . There must be a way to bring their cases before both state and federal courts."

To do so, blacks needed lawyers who were committed to the cause of winning constitutional rights for African Americans. Such lawyers were not to be found in abundance among white people. More African-American attorneys had to be trained to represent their people in the courts of the nation, and Dr. Mordecai Johnson, president of Howard University in Washington, D.C., determined to make Howard a cradle of black constitutional law talent. He was urged to do so by none other than Justice Louis Brandeis of the United States Supreme Court. In 1929, Johnson hired Charles Hamilton Houston as the new vice dean of Howard University Law School with the order to create a first-class institution.

Houston, born in 1895, a year before the *Plessy* decision, was a native of Washington, D.C., and had earned his law degree from Harvard University Law School. He hired black professors — among them his cousin, William Hastie, who had also graduated from Harvard Law School — to replace the previously all-white faculty, reduced the enrollment from eighty part-time students to thirty-seven full-time ones, and added courses in constitutional law to the basic law courses. Johnson himself taught the first civil rights law course at Howard, showing how the rights of personal liberty guaranteed in the Thirteenth and Fourteenth Amendments to the Constitution could be applied to the plight of black people.

The young and energetic black faculty at Howard Law School did not just teach. They also practiced their craft, and expected their students to help them in order to get hands-on experience in the law. In that atmosphere of both strong theoretical and practical learning, the students at Howard Law School thrived.

One of the best and brightest was Thurgood Marshall. Born in Baltimore, Maryland, in 1908, Marshall had earned his bachelor's degree at the all-black Lincoln University in Pennsylvania. Having decided to become a lawyer, he would have preferred to attend the law school at the University of Maryland, but that school did not accept black students. At Howard, he thrived under Charles Hamilton Houston and William Hastie, graduated at the top of his class in 1933, and joined a small black law firm in Baltimore. But he was bored with the practice of basic law.

In 1935, the NAACP decided to launch a full-scale campaign against legal injustices suffered by African-Americans. Charles Hamilton Houston was named to lead that campaign, and for help he turned to the young black attorneys he had helped groom at Howard. He named Thurgood Marshall the NAACP's legal counsel in Baltimore. In that capacity, Marshall helped a young black man named Donald Murray gain admittance to the previously all-white University of Maryland Law School. By 1936, Marshall had joined Charles Hamilton Houston at the NAACP in New York; and two years later, when Houston stepped down, Marshall was named chief counsel for the NAACP at its national headquarters in New York.

Houston retired in victory. In 1938, he had successfully argued before the United States Supreme Court in the case of *Gaines* v. *Missouri* that the state of Missouri either had to build a separate law school for blacks or desegregate the white law school. The Court clearly intended to uphold the letter of the separate-but-equal doctrine. The following year, the number of cases of all kinds the NAACP was pursuing across the country caused the organization to set up a separate legal branch; Thurgood Marshall was named director of the new Legal Defense and Education Fund.

In addition to pursuing equalization in education cases, Thurgood Marshall defended or organized the defense of blacks in capital cases, and represented plaintiffs in suits against segregation on interstate buses and in voting rights suits. After World War II broke out in Europe and the United States made ready to engage in the conflict, Marshall represented a black man named Yancey Williams, who wanted to join the new Army Air Corps, and succeeded in getting the army to train thirty-three black pilots to become the Ninety-ninth Pursuit Squadron.

Thousands of blacks served in the armed services, both on the home front and overseas, in an effort, it was said, "to make the world safe for democracy." When they returned home after the American and Allied victories over Nazi Germany and Japan, they were proud of their service and resentful that they did not enjoy at home the same rights they had sought to maintain for others. In the South, whites were concerned that the returning black soldiers had forgotten their "place" in Southern society, and it became dangerous for a black soldier to appear in public in uniform.

But even in the South, a change was beginning. World War II, a battle between the forces of democracy and the forces of totalitarianism, and the frightening rise of Nazi Germany, which had killed millions of Jews in an attempt to "purify" the German population, had been a bitter lesson of man's inhumanity to man. It was hard for white Americans to feel good about defeating the Nazis when Americans discriminated against and segregated darker-complected people in their own country.

Two American presidents had begun to take the first official steps against discrimination. In

Separate But Not Equal

Thousands of blacks served during World War II.

Nine members of the New York Women's Army Corps

1941, just after the United States entered World War II, President Franklin Delano Roosevelt had issued an executive order prohibiting discrimination by race, color, creed, or national origin in any defense plant that received contracts from the federal government. In 1946, after the war was over, Harry S Truman, who had become president upon the death of Roosevelt, set up the President's Commission on Civil Rights "to determine whether and in what respect . . . the authority and

President Harry Truman, Eleanor Roosevelt, and Walter White,
Executive Secretary of the NAACP, in 1947

means possessed by the federal, state, and local governments may be strengthened and improved to safeguard the rights of the people." The following June, he was the first American president ever to speak at an NAACP convention; and in 1948 he issued an executive order ending segregation in the United States armed forces.

Thurgood Marshall believed that with a president on the side of civil rights, it was time to push more aggressively for them. But some officials of the NAACP were not ready for bold action, and Marshall did not want to risk factionalizing the organization. He did, however, decide to concentrate on the area in which segregation bothered blacks the most — education — attacking the "separate but equal" educational opportunities that were clearly not equal at all.

Thurgood Marshall and the other NAACP attorneys began their campaign to secure equal education for blacks on the graduate-school level. In Oklahoma, Ada Lois Sipuel was denied admittance to the University of Oklahoma Law School because she was black. She went to the NAACP for help, and the case eventually went all the way to the United States Supreme Court, which ruled in her favor.

In the meantime, George McLaurin's application to the graduate program in education at the University of Oklahoma was rejected; he, too, sued, and a state court directed the university to admit him. The university complied with the court order but deliberately made conditions so uncomfortable for McLaurin that he would give up. He had to sit in a separate alcove in class and at a separate table in the cafeteria. He sued again, the case went up the American legal ladder to the Supreme Court, and the Court ordered the state to remove all restrictions against McLaurin as a student.

In Texas, Heman Sweatt was denied admission to the University of Texas Law School. Sweatt sued, and aware of what had happened in Oklahoma, the state hurriedly set up a separate black law school consisting of two rooms and one part-time instructor. Sweatt went to the NAACP for help, and the state moved the makeshift black law school to a building near the grounds of the state university and gave the black students access to the state law library (although not the university's law library). In effect, the school was now in compliance with the separate-but-equal doctrine.

Thurgood Marshall saw an opportunity to attack that doctrine directly.

As he was preparing his arguments, a group of white students at the University of Texas formed

Mrs. Daisy Bates, president of the Little Rock, Arkansas, chapter of the NAACP (center left), and Thurgood Marshall (center right), pictured in 1958 with six of the Little Rock Central High School Students on the steps of the Supreme Court

an all-white branch of the NAACP, which from its founding had been an integrated group, and began to hold demonstrations on campus in support of Sweatt. But the state courts rejected Sweatt's case, and again Thurgood Marshall found himself arguing before the United States Supreme Court. He won there again, the court concluding that no education under the circumstances at the University of Texas could be "substantially equal."

Groundwork

The Supreme Court decisions in *McLaurin* v. *Oklahoma State Regents for Higher Education* and *Sweatt* v. *Painter* were milestones, for they had established that in higher education there could be no segregation. But Thurgood Marshall knew that the real battleground in segregated education was at the elementary level. It was time to move to that real battleground.

In June 1950, three weeks after the crucial Supreme Court decisions were handed down, Marshall convened a conference of lawyers with the specific purpose of planning an all-out legal attack on school segregation. The conference issued a resolution that all future education cases would seek "education on a nonsegregated basis and that no relief other than that will be acceptable." Actually, the conference, and the resolution that came out of it, simply formalized what NAACP attorneys were already doing. By June 1950, five key cases in which the aim was to dismantle the separate-but-equal doctrine as it applied to education were already in the works.

8.

Clarendon County, South Carolina

In 1947, Clarendon County, South Carolina, had a population of around 32,000. Seven out of every ten people were black. There were 4,000 farms in the county, less than a quarter of them belonging to blacks. But blacks in overwhelming numbers worked the land, either as tenant farmers or sharecroppers. In fact, Clarendon County, South Carolina, was the closest thing to the old Plantation South one could find in the middle of the twentieth century.

Its attitudes about education were also outdated. While during Reconstruction South Carolina had been among the most forward-looking states as regards education and the general public welfare, once Reconstruction ended it returned more quickly than other Southern states to pre-Civil War values. Not until 1915 had the state legislature passed laws to control child labor and to establish compulsory education.

In South Carolina, taxes supported the schools. As tenant farmers and sharecroppers, blacks made very little money and so paid comparatively little

Classroom in rural Alabama in 1965

in taxes. That was the reason most frequently cited for why their children had such poor schools. According to the whites who controlled the local government on all levels, since white people paid the taxes, the white people were entitled to the better schools.

In Clarendon County, for the school year

1949–1950, $179 was spent for every white child, $43 for every black. There were sixty-one small, ramshackle buildings called schools for blacks, twelve substantial school facilities for whites. There were thirty school buses for white children, none for black children. When the black parents asked the white chairman of the school board, R. W. Elliot, for a bus, Elliot answered, "We ain't got no money to buy a bus for your nigger children." So the black parents pooled their resources and bought a secondhand bus. They then approached Elliot to ask if the county would provide gasoline for the bus. Again, they were denied.

Joseph Albert DeLaine, called J. A., a local black minister and schoolteacher, knew that the NAACP was looking for test cases against school desegregation. Quietly, because he feared losing his teaching job if he were found out, he approached several black parents about suing the Clarendon County School Board on the issue of equal transportation. Among those who agreed to help was a man named Levi Pearson, who owned his own farm. In fact, Pearson agreed to be the official plaintiff in the case of *Pearson* v. *County Board of Education*. The suit was thrown out of court after it was found that Pearson had no legal standing in the case, for his farm was almost exactly on the line between two different school districts. But that did not prevent local whites from retaliating against Pearson. No white-owned store or bank would give him credit. To raise cash to buy seed, he cut down some of his timber; but the mill, owned by R. W. Elliott, would not buy it.

In March 1949, DeLaine and Pearson attended a meeting in Columbia, South Carolina, called by Thurgood Marshall. Marshall told the men that the NAACP wanted to seek equal treatment in all aspects of public education, from buses to buildings, from equipment to teachers' salaries. If they could find twenty plaintiffs who were willing to take on the bigger issues, the NAACP would bring a major test case there. In the meantime, the school board fired J. A. DeLaine from his teaching job.

It took eight months, but the twenty people were found, and the campaign began. Since his name was first in alphabetical order, Harry Briggs received the dubious honor of having the case named after him. Harry Briggs lost his job at a local service station; his wife was fired from her job as a motel chambermaid, even though her name was not on the petition. Other petitioners also suffered. J. A. DeLaine urged them not to give up the fight.

J. A. DeLaine and his family were in for the worst reprisals. His wife, two of his sisters, and a niece lost their jobs. One of the churches at which he pastored was stoned, then later burned to the ground. His house also burned to the ground as men from the closest fire department stood and watched, insisting that his house was not in their jurisdiction.

DeLaine received repeated death threats. One night, shotgun fire erupted around the DeLaines' house. DeLaine fired back and called the police, but no one came. So he jumped into his car and fled, driving north across the state line. In his absence, he was charged, for having shot back that night, with felonious assault with a deadly weapon, and so he became an official fugitive from justice. Eventually, the charges were dropped.

Thurgood Marshall and other NAACP attorneys were keenly aware of the dangers the plaintiffs faced; and because of those dangers, they felt they had to pursue the case, even though it was not one they would have chosen. They wanted to attack the doctrine of "separate but equal." But they did not believe the Briggs case was the way to do it. After all, to push not just for equalization but for integration in Clarendon County would mean asking the integration of a population of white children that was less than half the size of the population of black children. For this case, the NAACP at first tried to return to its earlier strategy of attacking the inequality of separate facilities. But it was clear that segregation itself was at issue.

Under the Judiciary Act of 1937, cases that challenged the constitutionality of a state law were tried before special, three-judge federal district courts. Thurgood Marshall believed that two of the three judges who would hear the case were fair-minded, good men. Perhaps this case would get a fair hearing.

To attack segregation itself, Marshall had to show that it was an example of man's inhumanity to man. The idea behind the *Plessy* decision had been that blacks were by nature inferior and that separate but equal simply recognized that fact and made it the basis of law. Marshall's task was to prove that blacks were not by nature inferior to whites and that to subject them to inferior conditions was damaging to them as human beings.

Since the 1920s, there had been a growing body of work in the fields of psychology and sociology that debunked the so-called scientific bases of racism. At the urging of his colleague Robert Carter and against the warnings of other colleagues that if he departed from the sphere of law he was asking for trouble, Marshall decided to use some of that work in his arguments.

*Dr. Kenneth B. Clark played an important role in the fight
for desegregation.*

In the *Briggs* case, Carter and Marshall asked
the black psychologist Dr. Kenneth Clark to testify
about the work he and his wife, Mamie Phipps
Clark, also a psychologist, had done with children
and the effects of race on their sense of identity.

The Clarks had conducted studies in Washington, D.C., at first, then moved to New York, and eventually established the Northside Center for Child Development.

To measure children's self-esteem as it related to race, the Clarks devised what became known as the doll test. They showed four identical dolls, two white and two brown, to black children ages three to seven. After establishing that the children knew the differences in color, they made such requests of the children as "Give me the doll you like best" or "Give me the doll that is the nice doll" or "Give me the doll that looks bad." Even the three-year-olds showed an unmistakable preference for the white dolls.

Other psychologists had conducted even more ambitious and extensive tests, using cardboard dolls, clothing, and houses with both black and white children. Their findings had corroborated those of the Clarks.

What the tests revealed was that the sense of racial inferiority was instilled early, and that if it were not addressed in the early years, it would be fixed forever as a determinant of despair and self-hatred.

At Marshall's request, Clark conducted doll tests with sixteen black children (ages six to nine) in Clarendon County. Their responses were the same as the Clarks had found elsewhere.

The *Briggs* case was heard by the three-judge United States District Court in May 1951. Attorneys for the state startled Marshall and his team momentarily by listing all the measures the state of South Carolina had recently undertaken to make separate educational facilities more equal. Indeed, the state had recently formed a commission to look into school funding issues; and there were more attempts in the works to bring about parity in facilities so as to head off attacks against segregation itself. But the NAACP attorneys were having none of this late-in-the-day finagling.

In addition to Clark, other social scientists testified that segregation was damaging to young minds. Marshall hammered away at the argument that separate facilities were unconstitutional. But two of the three judges had no intention of overruling the precedent of *Plessy* v. *Ferguson*. In his dissent, the one antisegregationist, Judge J. Waties Waring, insisted that *Briggs* had nothing to do with *Plessy* v. *Ferguson*, which had dealt with segregation on railroads, not in schools.

The NAACP attorneys were not surprised. They immediately appealed the decision to the United States Supreme Court.

9.

Topeka, Kansas

Well before the *Briggs* decision came down, Thurgood Marshall and his staff were hurrying to complete arrangements for school desegregation suits in other communities. Their plan was to return to the Supreme Court with a suit that combined several communities and showed that wherever school segregation occurred, and however it varied from one community to another, it was pervasive and unjust.

One community to which they looked was not in the South but rather in the West — in Kansas, which, when the question of its statehood had arisen in the early nineteenth century, had been one of the battlefields between proslavery and antislavery forces in Congress.

As the fight over slavery heated up in the middle years of the nineteenth century, Kansas, which at the time was part of the Western frontier, became a particular battleground. The Missouri Compromise of 1820 had established the southern border of Missouri as the northernmost limit of slave territory. But while Kansas was above the northernmost limit, and while its climate did not support the large plantations that were the backbone of slavery, nevertheless slave owners and proslavery advocates began to settle there and establish slavery in defiance of the compromise. In response, New England abolitionist groups began to sponsor the creation of antislavery communities, among them Topeka. In 1854, Congress passed the Kansas-Nebraska Act. It provided that both Kansas and Nebraska were to be organized as territories and that their respective legislatures should decide the question of slavery. The act set off a fierce struggle for control of the territorial legislature, and the territory came to be called "bleeding Kansas."

Kansas still had not been admitted to statehood when the Southern states seceded from the Union and the Civil War began. Shortly thereafter, it was admitted to statehood in the Union and contributed its manpower to the Union cause. But while it was officially antislavery, it was not problack. The very first territorial legislature had provided for separate schools for blacks in the larger communities; and in 1867, shortly after ratifying the Fourteenth Amendment, the state government had extended the concept of separate schools to smaller cities, including Topeka.

Topeka, Kansas

In 1903, a man named William Reynolds tried to enroll his son in a school set aside for whites in Topeka. After he was refused, he brought suit against the Board of Education. The state supreme court denied his suit, citing the United States Supreme Court decision in *Plessy* v. *Ferguson* as well as other state cases upholding school segregation. Not for forty-eight years would another black man try to buck the Topeka school system.

In 1951, Topeka, Kansas, did not have separate waiting rooms at train and bus stations, and blacks were not relegated to the backs of buses. But only one white movie theater admitted blacks, and they had to sit in the balcony; blacks were barred from the town swimming pool, from all its hotels, except the Dunbar, which was for blacks, and from most of its restaurants, except as take-out customers. There were eighteen schools for whites and four for blacks, who made up 7½ percent of the population.

Oliver Brown and his family lived on First Street near the Topeka Avenue viaduct, over which trains rumbled at all times of the day. In fact, First Street was bisected by railroad tracks. The neighborhood was ethnically mixed — mostly white, with black, Mexican, and Indian families. When Brown's eldest daughter, Linda Carol, started school, she could not attend the all-white Sumner

Linda Brown, age nine

School, a three-block walk from her home. Rather, she had to go to the Monroe School, which was for colored children, about a mile away. To get to school by 9 A.M., Linda had to leave her house at 7:40. She had to walk between the train tracks for six blocks down First Street and through the dangerous Rock Island Line switching yards to get to the bus pickup point at the corner of Quincy Street by 8 A.M. Often the bus was late, and she had to wait at the pickup point in all kinds of weather. When the bus was on time, the thirty-minute trip deposited her at school half an hour early, and she was forced to wait outside until the school opened at 9 A.M.

The summer Linda was seven, registration notices for the Sumner School were stuck in the door of every home on First Street. Oliver Brown knew they were not for his children, but he was fed up with the dangerous commute his oldest daughter had to make every day. That September, he took her to the Sumner School. When his attempt to register her was refused, he contacted the NAACP, and the suit that became known as *Brown* v. *Board of Education of Topeka* began.

As in the other cases, Linda Brown was not the only plaintiff. Several black Topekans joined the suit, and *Brown* v. *Board of Education of Topeka* was actually a cluster of cases. The issue was not simply school location and the conditions of commuting. It was also the quality of the schools for blacks as compared to the schools for whites. And, most importantly, it was about how separate schools were psychologically damaging to black children. Several psychologists and professors of psychology testified at the behest of the NAACP. But the case, which eventually went before the United States Court of Appeals for the Tenth Circuit, presided over by Judge Walter August Huxman, was decided against the NAACP and the black plaintiffs it represented.

The court held that the precedent established in *Plessy* v. *Ferguson* had not been overruled and that it "presently" continued to be "authority for the maintenance of the segregated school system in the lower grades." But while the appeals court judges did not feel the *Brown* case was strong enough to overturn *Plessy*, they wanted to make clear their conclusion that segregation was injurious to black children. Added on to the court's opinion were nine "Findings of Fact" in the case. One of these findings supported the testimony that had been given by psychologists testifying for the NAACP:

"Segregation of white and colored children in public schools has a detrimental effect upon the

Outside the U.S. Supreme Court, people lined up hoping to be admitted to hear arguments on the issue of segregation.

colored children. The impact is greater when it has the sanction of the law; for the policy of separating the races is usually interpreted as denoting the inferiority of the Negro group. A sense of inferiority affects the motivation of a child to learn. Segregation with the sanction of law, therefore, has a tendency to retard the educational and mental development of Negro children and to deprive them of some of the benefits they would receive in a racially integrated school system."

Despite its loss in the case, the NAACP attorneys were delighted with those Findings of Fact. It seemed to them that Judge Huxman had deliberately challenged the United States Supreme Court to revisit *Plessy* v. *Ferguson*. Years later, Judge Huxman admitted that this was exactly his intention: "We weren't in sympathy with the decision we rendered," he said in 1970. "If it weren't for *Plessy* v. *Ferguson*, we surely would have found the law unconstitutional. But there was no way around it — the Supreme Court had to overrule itself."

10.

Delaware

Although Delaware, the first of the states to have ratified the Constitution, is located mostly above the Mason-Dixon line, and had remained in the Union when the Southern states seceded, it was to all intents and purposes a Southern state. In fact, it had refused to ratify the three post-Civil War amendments that were aimed at establishing blacks as full citizens: the Thirteenth, Fourteenth, and Fifteenth. (Ratification by two thirds of the states was needed for the amendments to become the law of the land, so Delaware was outvoted.) These refusals boded ill for the African Americans within its borders. The state did not even pay lip service to the idea of equality.

State requirements that voters must be property owners, as well as poll taxes, kept most blacks from voting. The separate colored schools were paid for largely by a tax levied against African Americans, which guaranteed that the schools would be underfunded. The school year for whites was twice as long as it was for blacks. As late as

1920, 20 percent of blacks in Delaware were illiterate, as compared to less than 2 percent of whites. In 1950, when blacks constituted 14 percent of the state's population, there was not a single four-year high school for blacks in the entire state. And Delaware State College for Negroes, like many similar colleges in other states, was little more than a glorified high school.

In 1949, thirty students at Delaware State applied to the all-white University of Delaware and were rejected. They then took their case to Louis Redding, who had made a reputation for himself as a top-notch lawyer who was willing to represent the interests of his people. With Jack Greenberg, a young white lawyer who had just joined the NAACP legal department established by Thurgood Marshall, Redding took the case to Delaware's Chancery Court, which had jurisdiction over such issues as the custody of children, the guardianship of old people, the pardoning of criminals, and the civil rights of blacks. Vice-chancellor Collins Seitz found the colored college "grossly inferior" and ordered the black plaintiffs admitted to the white university, thus making the University of Delaware the first state-financed institution in the United States to be desegregated at the undergraduate level by court order.

Two years later, in June 1951, over considerable opposition from Delaware racists, Collins Seitz was named chancellor of Delaware. Four months later, he presided over one of the four state cases brought by the NAACP against segregated schools.

The NAACP case in Delaware was actually two cases, *Belton* v. *Gebhart* and *Bulah* v. *Gebhart.* Francis B. Gebhart was the member of the State Board of Education whose name was alphabetically first. Belton was Ethel Louis Belton, who with seven other black parents wanted their children admitted to the local white high school in Claymont, a town north of Wilmington, rather than have them bused downtown to Wilmington's colored Howard High School. Bulah was Sarah Bulah of Hockessin, a rural village west of Wilmington. She protested the fact that she had to drive her daughter, Shirley, two miles to a one-room schoolhouse for colored children when a bus passed right by her front door, transporting white children to the white school just up the hill. Sarah Bulah's first aim was to get a bus for the black children. But when she approached Louis Redding about her case, he suggested a broader protest. As she told Richard Kluger, author of *Simple Justice,* "He said he wouldn't help me get a Jim Crow bus to take my girl to any Jim Crow school, but if I was interested

*In 1961, Jack Greenberg replaced Thurgood Marshall as
NAACP Chief Counsel.*

in sendin' her to an integrated school, then maybe
he'd help. Well, I thanked God right then and
there."

Redding, again working with the white
NAACP attorney Jack Greenberg, decided that the
two cases combined were an opportunity to attack
the principle of school segregation. In planning

their arguments, the attorneys decided to focus heavily on the social and psychological effects of legal segregation as it applied to education. Dr. Kenneth Clark was asked to conduct his doll tests with a group of forty-one black youngsters in Delaware. Based on these tests, Clark asserted even more boldly than he had at the Charleston, South Carolina, trial five months earlier that school segregation impaired the overall functioning of black children. He testified that 100 percent of the children had correctly identified themselves with the brown doll and that three out of four, when asked the question "Which of these dolls is likely to act bad?" had picked the brown doll. He said in the Chancery Court, "I think we have clear-cut evidence of rather deep damage to the self-esteem of these youngsters, a feeling of inferiority, a feeling of inadequacy — evidence which was further supported by the kind of things which the youngsters said: 'I suppose we do act kind of bad. We don't act like white people.'"

Testimony as to the psychological damage caused by segregation was also given by Dr. Frederic Wertheim, a prominent white clinical psychiatrist from Europe who ran a clinic in Harlem, and a number of other people.

In response, the state of Delaware did not mount a very convincing case. The state superintendent in charge of the Department of Public Instruction could only point to an act of the state legislature three months earlier that had assured equal per capita spending for white and black schoolchildren, which in theory should have been done after the *Plessy* v. *Ferguson* decision fifty-five years earlier.

Chancellor Seitz listened to the testimony, and personally visited both white and black schools in the Wilmington area. He ruled in the case that the black schools were dismally inferior. He did not attempt to overturn the constitutionality of *Plessy* (that was up to the United States Supreme Court), but he concluded that the practice of racial separation "creates a mental health problem in many Negro children with a resulting impediment to their educational progress."

Seitz concluded his opinion by saying that it was not enough that the state now intended to make the separate schools equal. "It seems to me that when a plaintiff shows to the satisfaction of the court that there is an existing and continuing violation of the 'separate but equal' doctrine, he is entitled to have made available to him the state facilities which have been shown to be superior. To do otherwise is to say to such a plaintiff, 'Yes, your Constitutional rights are being invaded, but be patient, we will see whether in time they are still be-ing violated.'" He ruled that Shirley Barbara Bulah in Hockessin and the children of Ethel Louise Bel-ton and the other plaintiffs in Claymont were enti-tled to immediate admission to the white schools in their communities. Thus, for the first time, seg-regated white elementary and high schools in the United States were ordered by a court of law to ad-mit black children. A jubilant Thurgood Marshall announced to the press, "This is the first real vic-tory in our campaign to destroy segregation of American pupils in elementary and high schools."

11.

Virginia

Virginia, the site of most of the famous battles of the Civil War, emerged from the war devastated. It was also about one third smaller, for during the war, in 1863, a portion of the state had seceded to form West Virginia, which then refused to be responsible for any of Virginia's huge debt. Besides being viewed as a dictatorship, the postwar Reconstruction occupation by Union troops and the government of Northerners, Southern sympathizers, and blacks was also resented for its measures to provide a costly free public school system.

After Reconstruction, like the other states of the former Confederacy, Virginia moved quickly to restore "normal life." A literacy test was instituted as a requirement for voting, and tight restrictions were placed on state-supported services such as health and education. By the 1920s, the state's huge debt had been paid off and its economy was booming.

The First World War had contributed greatly to Virginia's prosperity. The port city of Norfolk became the chief East Coast base for the United States Navy, and neighboring Newport News became a major shipbuilding center. The arrival of new workers finally spurred some improvements in services, including education, but it took some time for these improvements to reach the interior of the state.

In Prince Edward County, a small, rural area in south central Virginia, it was not until the 1920s that the county officials established two high schools for white children. Black children had to wait until 1939 for theirs. Robert R. Moton High

A school in rural Georgia in 1941

School was named for the most famous black man to have been born in the county, the man who had succeeded Booker T. Washington as principal of Tuskegee Institute. It was separate but not equal. It had no gymnasium, cafeteria, or auditorium with fixed seats, all of which the larger of the two white high schools, Farmville High, had. While students at Farmville High could take subjects such as physics, world history, geography, trigonometry, and Latin, as well as such vocational subjects as shorthand, woodwork, machine shop, electricity, and mechanical drawing, none of these subjects was available to the students at Moton High. Its teachers were paid less, and its supplies were fewer. And by 1947, with an enrollment double that for which it had been built, it was severely overcrowded. Three wooden buildings with tar-paper roofs were built adjacent to the school; they were heated with stoves. The African-American parents were angry that their children were forced to try to learn in "shacks."

The Reverend Francis Griffin, pastor of the First Baptist Church in Farmville, knew about the NAACP's campaign for equal schools. He gathered together the required fifty people to start a chapter of the NAACP in Prince Edward County and contacted Spottswood Robinson and Oliver Hill, two black NAACP attorneys in Richmond. Working with the Moton High School PTA, Griffin, as president of the local NAACP chapter, petitioned the school board several times in 1950 and 1951 for a new colored high school. But while the board expressed willingness to help, it did nothing.

Barbara Johns was by then a junior at Moton, and fed up with the conditions at her school. In April 1951, she organized a student strike. The students announced that they would go to school each day for the remainder of the school year. But they would stay outside carrying picket signs. Or, if they were inside, at their desks, they would not open their books. The students did not have the approval of most of their parents, nor of the school principal, but Barbara Johns and her fellow students were undeterred. With the assistance of the Reverend Griffin, they wrote to the NAACP in Richmond for help.

Oliver Hill and Spottswood Robinson, both products of Howard University Law School, were in favor of the NAACP's new tactic of attacking segregation itself. But they wanted to launch it in a large city, not in some rural, sparsely populated, deeply racist county. However, they told Barbara Johns and her fellow students that they would get involved in their case, provided that they sue for the end of segregation itself, not just a new school. Moreover, their parents would have to be solidly behind legal action aimed at this eventuality. A mass meeting was held at the Reverend Griffin's church on May 3, and the parents voted overwhelmingly to support a legal suit. They were somewhat ashamed that their own children had been forced to take action in the wake of their inactivity.

The suit was filed in Richmond on May 23, 1951. Alphabetically, the first name on the list of students was a fourteen-year-old ninth grader named Dorothy E. Davis, and the case was called *Davis* v. *County School Board of Prince Edward County*.

In the slow pace of court proceedings, the matter did not come to trial for six months. In the meantime, Barbara Johns was sent for her safety to stay with her uncle, the Reverend Vernon Johns, pastor of Dexter Avenue Baptist Church in Montgomery, Alabama. Some years earlier, while living in Prince Edward County, Virginia, the Reverend Johns had led a successful campaign for school buses for Negro children. It was fitting that his niece should have later led a student strike against unequal schools there. As outspoken in Montgomery, Alabama, as he had been in Prince Edward

County, the Reverend Johns would soon be forced by racist whites to leave Alabama. His place as pastor of Dexter Avenue Baptist Church would be taken by a young minister named Martin Luther King, Jr.

The Farmville case now concerned far more than the matter of a new colored high school. It was about equal education — about the outdoor toilets at the colored elementary schools in the county, about the fact that the man who drove the bus that took Barbara Johns to school also built the fires in the tar-paper shacks and then took up his duties as the high school history teacher. The NAACP lawyers sought to have the Prince Edward County colored schools declared unequal and the Virginia segregation statute declared unconstitutional.

Unlike Delaware, the state of Virginia mounted a spirited defense against this threat to its traditional way of life, a big part of which was the legally determined inferiority of black people.

The trial opened in United States District Court on February 25, 1952, in a special three-judge district court presided over by Judge Armistead Mason Dobie, seventy-one, who had a history of carefully reasoned decision making and few of whose decisions were ever overruled by higher courts.

These victims of racial segregation in Prince Edward County, Virginia, figured prominently in the NAACP's suit against the state of Virginia.

Among the expert witnesses called by the plaintiffs was a thirty-three-year-old social scientist, M. Brewster Smith, chair of the psychology department of Vassar College. Smith testified that there was a growing body of evidence that environmental rather than racial heritage was the prime factor in a student's learning ability. When asked why intelligence tests showed a considerable gap between whites and blacks, Smith answered that the gap was in achievement, not necessarily in capacity. After Smith testified that segregation was insulting to blacks, he was asked if it would not be insulting to the white people of Virginia if their customs were stripped away from them. Smith replied that he did not see why it was insulting. Asked what might happen if Southerners decided to ignore a court order to end segregation on grounds that the great majority of fellow citizens preferred to retain the practice, Smith answered, ". . . what we know of the psychology of prejudice leads us to believe that if a clear-cut, straightforward change is proposed from the height [i.e., the courts], that the population is very likely to go along with it, rather than with a gradual, pussyfooting sort of approach that in no way speaks firmly to those who are most deeply prejudiced. . . ."

Attorneys for the state of Virginia pointed out that there was segregation in the North, prejudice against blacks by whites in the North, and prejudice against darker-skinned Negroes by lighter-skinned ones. The state also called three psychologists as witnesses, among them Professor Henry Garrett, chairman of the psychology department at Columbia University in New York City. Coincidentally, Professor Garrett had taught both Dr. Kenneth Clark (who had also testified in the case) and his wife, Mamie Phipps Clark, at Columbia. In fact, Clark was at the counsel table with the NAACP attorneys when Garrett testified. Garrett was a native of Halifax County, Virginia; and not only his early experiences but also his later studies had convinced him that the Negro was inferior to the white man and that segregation was in the best interests of both races. However, when asked if he felt racial segregation was detrimental to the individual, even Garrett admitted, "In general, whenever a person is cut off from the main body of a society or group, if he is put in a position that stigmatizes him and makes him feel inferior, I would say yes, it is detrimental and deleterious to him."

In spite of this testimony, the three-judge district court panel ruled unanimously that racial separation in Virginia rested "neither upon prejudice nor caprice nor upon any other measureless foundation" but had "for generations been a part of the customs and mores of her people. To have separate schools has been their use and want."

12.

The Supreme Court Decides

By the fall of 1952, the United States Supreme Court had five school desegregation cases before it. The Court decided to group them together as one case. The fifth, which concerned segregation in Washington, D.C., was later separated out from the rest because Washington, D.C., was a federal district, not a state. The five cases were combined under the title *Brown* v. *Board of Education of Topeka*. It was ironic that the Supreme Court chose the Kansas case to represent, at least in name, the group of suits, for Kansas had little interest in defending its case. In fact, the Supreme Court virtually had to order the state attorney general of Kansas to participate.

The United States Supreme Court had many cases to hear and decide. The justices preferred to make their decisions based on written materials, known as briefs. They also heard oral arguments but imposed very strict time limits. Each side had one hour to present its case. For the NAACP, the preparation for that one hour took months of intensive work. Its lawyers, together with a host of advisers, argued heatedly over what testimony to concentrate on. There was great disagreement over whether to rely on the social science testimony. Dr. Kenneth Clark was asked to prepare a summary of the social science evidence relevant to the case; and in his carefully researched document he showed that there was a substantial body of evidence to show the adverse effects of segregation, not only on black students but also on whites. In whites, it produced "a distorted sense of social reality" as well as "moral cynicism." The NAACP attorneys then sent the statement to dozens of social scientists and asked that they sign it to signify their support. They received thirty-five signatures.

Thurgood Marshall arrived in the District ten days before the arguments. He wanted to be rested and "loose." He had argued before the Supreme Court fifteen times before and had won thirteen times. At nearby Howard University, he and the other attorneys, assisted by students, faculty, and outside advisers, held mock sessions that functioned as dry runs.

At last the day came. The Supreme Court heard the *Brown* case first, argued by Robert Carter for the NAACP and Paul Wilson, assistant attorney general for Kansas. Next came the *Briggs* case, argued by Thurgood Marshall for the NAACP and John W. Davis for the state of South Carolina. Spottswood Robinson argued in *Davis* v. *County School Board of Prince Edward County,* followed by Justin Moore of Richmond for Virginia. Historical considerations consumed much of the oral argument in the Washington, D.C., case, *Bolling* v. *Sharp.* James Nabrit of the NAACP shared oral arguments with a black Washington attorney named George Edward Chalmers Hayes. Milton Korman took the opposing side for the District. In the fifth and last of the combined school cases, Attorney General Albert Young of Delaware went first because he had lost in the state courts and was now the appellant, or the one who appeals. Louis Redding and Jack Greenberg, NAACP cocounsels, argued against him.

The Court that convened on the morning of December 13, 1952, to deliberate the matter of school segregation consisted of nine justices with some things in common and many differences among them. All nine had been appointed by Democratic presidents Franklin D. Roosevelt and Harry S Truman. Eight of the nine were themselves Democrats. Four were from the South, two from the Northeast, two from the Midwest, and one from the West. They were deeply divided over the issue of the constitutionality of segregation.

In fact, by late May 1953, the justices were hopelessly divided. On June 8, all five segregation cases were unanimously restored to the Court's calendar for reargument on October 12. The Court ordered new arguments in two areas: 1) the original intention of the Fourteenth Amendment; and 2) assuming that *Plessy* violated the Fourteenth Amendment, how would desegregation proceed?

To discover whether or not the Fourteenth Amendment intended to prohibit all forms of state-imposed racial discrimination meant reading old newspapers and court documents, autobiographies of congressmen of the time, notes from private meetings, and state archival records. But Thurgood Marshall barely batted an eyelash. He immediately set about coordinating the huge research project.

That September, Chief Justice Fred Vinson died of a heart attack at the age of sixty-three. No one will know for sure how he would have voted in the *Brown* case, but fellow justice Stanley Reed, who at the time was leaning toward upholding *Plessy* on the belief that there should be no "government by judges," later stated that he felt that Vinson and at least one other justice were prepared to agree with him.

Supreme Court Chief Justice Earl Warren

President Dwight D. Eisenhower, the World War II general who had won the presidency in 1952 as a Republican, although he was so popular and so above politics that he could also have been elected if he had run on the Democratic line, now had his first opportunity to name a Supreme Court Justice — and at a time when the Court faced one of the momentous decisions in a segregation case. He chose Earl Warren, the Republican governor of California. In Eisenhower's opinion, Warren, who was moderately progressive in his social philosophy, had the respect and confidence of the public.

Nominations to the Supreme Court must be confirmed by the Senate. Because Congress was in recess until the first of the year, Eisenhower appointed Warren to the Court on an interim basis. After Congress reconvened, Warren was confirmed as the fourteenth chief justice of the highest court in the land. His appointment would prove to be Eisenhower's main contribution to civil rights.

When the Court convened to hear rearguments in the *Brown* case in December, the elderly South Carolina attorney John W. Davis stated that the "South was confident of its good faith and intention to produce equality for all of its children of whatever race or color" and that "Your honors do not sit, and cannot sit, as a glorified board of education for the state of South Carolina or any other state." When he finished, the eighty-year-old attorney believed his argument would win on the question of law alone. He did not understand that the case was not being decided in a vacuum, that there were social and political events swirling around it that were bound to affect it.

Thurgood Marshall's arguments were not delivered in so courtly a fashion, nor were they as polished and precise. But they contained the ring of common sense. Davis had implied that black and white children could not possibly attend school together. Marshall wanted to know why they couldn't. "Those same kids in Virginia and South Carolina — and I have seen them do it — they play together in the streets together, they play on their farms together, they go down the road together, they separate to go to school, they come out of school and play ball together. They have to be separated in school.

"There is some magic to it. You can have them voting together, you can have them not restricted because of law in the houses they live in. You can have them going to the same state university and the same college, but if they go to elementary and high school, the world will fall apart. . . ." The only way the Court could uphold school segregation, said Marshall, was "to find that for some reason Negroes are inferior to all other human beings."

But the most memorable lines on behalf of the NAACP were spoken by James Nabrit when he said, "Our Constitution has no provision across it that all men are equal but that white men are more equal than others."

The arguments concluded, the Court met to discuss the case. In the opinion of the new chief justice, Earl Warren, it was a simple case. Over the years, many judicial decisions had chipped away at *Plessy*. The doctrine of separate but equal had been eroded to the extent that only the fact remained. The doctrine rested on the idea of the inferiority of the black race. He was very clear in discussions with the other justices how he wanted the decision to come out. Since four of the justices had indicated a year earlier that they were inclined to rule against separate-but-equal education, the majority of five was in place. But Warren understood that on such a momentous issue, the Court could not appear to be deeply divided. The justices had to present a united front and rule unanimously. But he did not push too hard until he was confirmed by the Senate, which occurred after the turn of the year and five months after he had joined the Court.

Sometime between late February and late March, the Court voted on the school-segregation cases. There exist no records of the vote, for the justices understood the extreme sensitivity of the case and didn't want any word to leak out. It is probable that at least two and possibly three were inclined not to overrule separate but equal; but Earl Warren and others managed to persuade them.

Supreme Court opinions were always announced on Mondays. On Monday, May 17, 1954, Chief Justice Earl Warren first read the Court's opinions in several other cases. He then announced that an opinion had been rendered in the *Brown* case. The four cases (that of the District of Columbia had been decided separately because it was not a state) had reached the Court by different routes but had been consolidated because each dealt with "minors of the Negro race" who had sought admission to public schools closed to them under "the so-called 'separate-but-equal' doctrine announced by this Court in *Plessy* v. *Ferguson*." The Court, the chief justice said, had first heard arguments about the specific cases and then rearguments about the meaning and intent of the Fourteenth Amendment. Those rearguments, said Warren, had not much helped the Court resolve

On Monday, May 17, 1954, Chief Justice Earl Warren announced the Supreme
Court's ruling on school segregation.

the issue. One reason was "the primitive nature of public education at the time of its adoption." There was "little in the history of the Fourteenth Amendment relating to its intended effect on public education.

"In approaching this problem, we cannot turn the clock back to 1868 when the Amendment was adopted, or even to 1896 when *Plessy* v. *Ferguson* was written. We must consider public education in the light of its full development and its present place in American life throughout the Nation. . . .

"Today, education is probably the most important function of state and local governments. Compulsory school attendance laws and the great expenditures for education both demonstrate our recognition of the importance of education to our democratic society. It is required in the performance of our most basic public responsibilities, even service in the armed forces. It is the very foundation of good citizenship. . . .

". . . To separate [black children] from others of similar age and qualifications solely because of their race generates a feeling of inferiority as to their status in the community that may affect their hearts and minds in a way unlikely ever to be undone."

The Warren opinion then mentioned *Plessy* directly. In *Plessy*, the Court had said essentially that inferiority was only in the mind of the Negro. "Whatever may have been the extent of psychological knowledge at the time of *Plessy* v. *Ferguson,* this finding [in the Kansas court in *Brown* that segregation denotes inferiority and diminishes the motivation to learn] is amply supported by modern authority. Any language in *Plessy* v. *Ferguson* contrary to this finding is rejected.

"We conclude," the chief justice read, "unanimously," he added, although that was not in the written opinion, "that in the field of public education the doctrine of 'separate but equal' has no place. Separate educational facilities are inherently unequal."

Warren then announced that at the beginning of the Court's fall term the justices would schedule further argument concerning how to apply the ruling.

In the Supreme Court chambers, and soon, across the country, there was instant recognition that this was a landmark decision that directly affected the lives of American families. It affirmed, at last, that the idea of equality for all on which the United States was founded included black people. The Court's decision was a recognition of American ideals.

Southern segregationists were furious. Thurgood Marshall and the other NAACP attorneys were overjoyed. Ordinary blacks were muted in their response, afraid to believe it, suspicious that it would somehow be undermined, reluctant to appear grateful for something they should have enjoyed all along.

They had good reason. It was more than a year before the Court issued a decree explaining how it wished the process of desegregation to occur. One reason for the delay was the death of Justice Robert Jackson, whom Eisenhower replaced with John Marshall Harlan, a New Yorker. There were two basic opposing arguments. One held that desegregation should proceed at once, by direct court order. This was Thurgood Marshall's argument. The other warned that such a tack would result in great civil unrest, and that individual localities should be given the right to follow the law in the way they thought best, which, in some localities, meant not in measurable time.

The Court adopted the more cautious choice. It remanded the matter to district courts, although it warned that "the vitality of these constitutional principles cannot be allowed to yield simply because of disagreement with them." The district courts should "take such proceedings and enter such orders and decrees consistent with this opinion as are necessary and proper to admit to public schools on a racially nondiscriminatory basis with all deliberate speed the parties to these cases."

That phrase "with all deliberate speed" would prove to be the salvation of the segregationists and the stumbling block for integration.

Thurgood Marshall and the NAACP lawyers knew that they faced more years of court battles. But this time the law of the land was on their side. As Marshall said to Carl Murphy of the Baltimore *Afro-American* shortly after the decision, "You can say all you want but those white crackers are going to get tired of having Negro lawyers beating 'em every day in court."

13.

Public Education in the Aftermath of *Brown*

The Supreme Court's *Brown* decision reached far beyond just schools. It set the stage for a change in American society and sparked a mass movement for civil rights. Within six months after the Court handed down its implementation decree, Rosa Parks of Montgomery, Alabama, was arrested for refusing to give up her seat on a city bus to a white man, sparking the Montgomery Bus Boycott, ably led by a young minister named Martin Luther, King, Jr., which succeeded in bringing about some improvements in conditions for blacks on the city's buses.

The direct-action civil rights movement followed. New organizations, such as King's Southern Christian Leadership Conference (SCLC) and the Student Nonviolent Coordinating Committee (SNCC), campaigned for civil rights in all areas of life by means of marches, sit-ins, voter-registration drives, and other forms of nonviolent protest.

In the meantime, NAACP attorneys kept up their campaign in the courts. In the twelve years

Martin Luther King, Jr., shaking hands with President Lyndon B. Johnson, who signed the Civil Rights Bill into law.

after *Brown,* the Supreme Court handed down decision after decision that outlawed segregation in public parks and recreation areas, on or at all interstate-transportation and interstate-commerce facilities, such as waiting rooms and lunch counters, as well as the buses and trains themselves, in libraries and courtrooms and the facilities of all public buildings, and in hotels, restaurants, and other public places.

Simultaneously, the executive and legislative branches of the federal government, following the lead of the judicial branch, passed a number of civil rights laws. During the administration of President Dwight D. Eisenhower, Congress passed the Civil Rights Act of 1957, the first such law since 1875. But the bill contained few provisions for enforcement and so paid only lip service to the idea of equality.

President John F. Kennedy, a Democrat, succeeded Eisenhower in the White House. He possessed a genuine and active commitment to civil rights and instructed his attorney general, who was also his brother, Robert F. Kennedy, to use the law to increase the pace of desegregation. Concurrently, the pace of direct-action civil rights campaigns in the South picked up. After the assassination of President Kennedy, his former vice president, Texan Lyndon B. Johnson, proclaimed his intention to carry on what his slain predecessor had started. During the Johnson administration, the Civil Rights Act of 1964 and the Voting Rights Act of 1965 were signed into law and remain today an effective standard of equality by which to measure discrimination. Whether they are used as a means to end discrimination and unequal practices has depended greatly on the administration in Washington, D.C.

Also in 1965, the passage of the Elementary and Secondary Education Act made sizable federal

A young demonstrator protests racism at the Selma, Alabama, civil rights march.

funds available to local school districts that complied with desegregation of schools under orders
of federal district courts. In 1968, the Fair Housing
Act made it unlawful to refuse to sell or rent to
anyone because of race or religion.

In 1961, President Kennedy had appointed Thurgood Marshall to the United States Court of Appeals for the Second Circuit. Six years later, in 1967, President Johnson nominated him for the United States Supreme Court. Confirmed by Congress, Thurgood Marshall, who more than any other living person had shepherded the legal campaign against separate-but-equal schools through the American legal system to victory, became the first African-American Supreme Court Justice. From that time until his death in 1993, Marshall was a strong voice on the Court for the rights of all individuals, not just African Americans. He also supported the idea that groups of people who had a long history of being treated unfairly deserved extra consideration and a little more help than those who had historically enjoyed greater advantages.

This concept, called "affirmative action," and first advanced during the Johnson administration, aimed to give an extra boost to both women and members of racial minority groups. While by the late 1960s all the legal mechanisms to ensure equality of opportunity were in place, centuries of discrimination had left most minority group members ill prepared to take advantage of the new opportunities. Under the concept of affirmative action, employers, college admissions officers, those who granted work contracts, and others in positions to select applicants, were expected to give preference to those who had historically been underrepresented.

President Johnson also declared a War on Poverty and pumped federal dollars into programs aimed at providing jobs, housing, and health and legal services to poor communities.

Meanwhile, desegregation of the formerly "separate but equal" schools did begin. The process was painful. Whites were extremely resistant to the change.

In theory, integration made perfect economic sense. Localities that had formerly practiced segregation would be able to spend their funds for education on one school system — one set of buildings, one faculty of principals and teachers, one inventory of books, sports equipment, and other supplies, one fleet of buses. But that is not what happened in many places. Whites, including some so-called white citizens councils, which were organizations dedicated to maintaining the separation of the races, established private, all-white academies. Although white parents had to pay tuition to send their children to these schools, many localities found ways (which were not entirely legal) to divert public funds to support the private academies. In some areas, the public schools became largely black, and because of the diversion of public education funds to the private academies, the public schools were left underfunded.

In those public schools, as many black teachers had feared, when it came time to integrate, and

Melba Patillo, one of the nine students to integrate Little Rock, Arkansas's, Central High School in 1957.

to choose between the black and the white teachers to staff them, it was the black teachers and principals who lost their jobs. Even some black teachers who did manage to stay in the system seemed to lose the sense of mission they'd had in the age of segregation. Many of the white teachers, unaccustomed to teaching black students, and prejudiced against them, made school life even more difficult for the black students.

The process was the most painful for the pioneering black students who were the first to integrate formerly all-white schools. In Little Rock, Arkansas, Melba Patillo, one of the nine students to integrate Central High in 1957, needed all the faith and courage she could muster to get through that year. In spite of the presence of United States Army soldiers, who were there specifically to protect her and the others, she was taunted unmercifully. White students would follow closely behind her as she walked in the hallways and step on her heels until they were sore and bleeding. Dynamite sticks were thrown at her. After a pep rally, as she moved with the rest of the crowd out of the school auditorium, she found herself being shoved into a corner by three or four football players. One of them pressed his forearm against her throat, choking her, and promised menacingly, "We're gonna make your life hell, nigger. Y'all are gonna go screaming out of here, taking those nigger-loving soldiers with you."

The terror continued unabated throughout that school year. The students could not imagine it getting worse but, as the year drew to a close, it did. Racist white students were determined that the nine would not finish out the school year. Racist white adults made dozens of threatening telephone calls to the students' homes. But the one senior, Ernest Green, would not be dissuaded from graduating with his class. Under heavy police guard, he was escorted to and from the graduation ceremonies. The other eight students did not attend, for fear of their safety.

The following September of 1958, the students, represented by the NAACP, won the right to reenter Central High. But Governor Orval Faubus closed all the city's high schools rather than allow integration to proceed. The schools remained shut for an entire year. During that time, two of the nine students' families moved away from Little Rock because of the pressure. The other students eventually went elsewhere to finish high school.

Not until September 1960 did legal victories by the NAACP force the reopening of Little Rock's high schools. Only two black students were allowed to enroll at Central High that year, but like Ernest Green before them, they managed to graduate.

Similar white resistance occurred throughout the South, but through additional Supreme Court rulings and federal action, school integration proceeded.

On the Supreme Court, Earl Warren served his last term as chief justice during the administration of President Richard Nixon. He and the rest of the Court made it clear that the stalling that resulted from the "deliberate speed" part of their 1955 ruling must end. They ruled in *Green* v. *County School Board of New Kent County, Virginia,* that the "freedom of choice" plans operating in many school districts were just new versions of segregation. Nixon hoped that his choice for Chief Justice, Warren E. Burger, would lead the Court on a less aggressive route. But Burger, too, supported desegregation without further delay. In the fall of 1969, in *Alexander* v. *Holmes County* (Mississippi) *Board of Education,* Burger wrote the unanimous opinion, in which he stated: "Under explicit holdings of this Court, the obligation of every school district is to terminate dual school systems at once and to operate now and hereafter only unitary schools."

Slowly, the Southern school districts complied, so that by the 1972–1973 school year, nearly half the black children in eleven Southern states were attending schools that were predominantly white. By the twentieth anniversary of the _Brown_ decision, there had been real progress in school desegregation in the South. More educational opportunities, combined with added legal rights in other areas of life, helped a segment of the African-American population. The black middle class grew, as the number of black college graduates and professionals in all areas increased. A significant black middle class developed in the South, where the

Two girls primping at bathroom mirrors in school in 1958.

booming economy and new opportunities for blacks in some urban areas led to the coining of the term *New South*.

Desegregation in the South, although difficult to accomplish, actually proved easier than desegregation in the North, where residential patterns created separate schools. Most blacks lived in predominantly black neighborhoods, most whites in predominantly white. The local schools reflected the composition of the neighborhood. In the post-World War II era, the cities became even more segregated. In the aftermath of the war, the United States government decided to reward the men and women who had fought in its armed services through the GI Bill. The GI Bill earmarked funds for former soldiers and sailors and pilots to attend college and to obtain low-interest loans to buy homes. Ambitious developers built huge tracts of inexpensive single-family homes outside the cities. The overwhelming majority of the new suburbanites were white. They left the cities, and the schools, to the blacks. In the North and West, in the 1972–1973 school year, only 28 percent of black children were enrolled at schools where whites were in the majority. This *de facto* segregation (segregation in fact) proved much more difficult to combat than legal segregation.

In order to comply with the Supreme Court's decision banning segregation, measures had to be taken to integrate the schools. The most used measure was busing. Black students could travel to

A first grader was the only child on a school bus taking pupils from a black school to a white one.

formerly all-white schools on buses, and white students could travel to formerly all-black schools.

It was not an ideal situation. Most parents, black and white, preferred that their children attend schools close to home. Whites had, of course, never objected to black students being bused miles away from their homes to black schools; but when it was white students being bused, that was a different matter. In the interests of integration, however, many state, local, and federal courts ordered school districts to institute busing programs.

While President Johnson was in office, many branches of the federal government worked to ensure compliance with the school antisegregation laws. The Department of Health, Education, and Welfare carefully monitored local communities to make sure school-desegregation guidelines were being met; if not, and if the districts did not take steps to remedy the situation, federal funds were cut off. The Johnson administration supported busing or whatever else it took to achieve integration. But after Johnson, beleaguered by the war in Vietnam and the growing antiwar movement in the United States, chose not to seek another term, Republican Richard M. Nixon became president. He called busing "forced integration," and his administration backed off on the school-desegregation issue. The Supreme Court continued to support busing, but the Court is made up of presidential appointees, and during his administration President Nixon had the opportunity to appoint more conservative justices.

In April 1971, the Court ruled unanimously in a school integration case, *Swann* v. *Charlotte-Mecklenburg* [North Carolina] *Board of Education,* that whatever steps were necessary to achieve integration should be taken. The opinion, written by Chief Justice Warren Burger, stated, in part, that all things being equal, it was best to assign pupils to the schools nearest their homes, but "all things are not equal in a system that has been deliberately constructed and maintained to enforce racial segregation."

During the 1972–1973 school year, the Supreme Court handed down a nearly unanimous ruling (Nixon appointee Justice William J. Rehnquist, dissented) in an NAACP Legal Defense Fund sponsored case, *Keys* v. *Denver School District No. 1.* The Court found that the school board had acted to intentionally segregate its system and ordered it to take steps to achieve integration.

But Nixon had appointed a total of four justices to the Supreme Court, and in the same school year, those four, joined by an Eisenhower appointee, Potter Stewart, refused to rule against methods of funding of public schools that were discriminatory. Most school districts relied on property taxes to pay for their public schools. That meant that in poorer areas, lower property taxes produced less money for schools. The disparity was especially evident in areas where predominantly white, affluent suburbs surrounded increasingly black and Latino inner cities. But in the case of *San Antonio Independent School District* v. *Rodriguez*, the Court would not find these methods of funding discriminatory. In essence, the Court approved unequal schools. Justice Thurgood Marshall wrote, in his dissenting opinion, "The majority's holding can only be seen as a retreat from our historic commitment to the equality of educational opportunity and as unsupportable acquiescence in a system which deprives children in their earliest years of the chance to reach their full potential as citizens."

In the case of *Milliken* v. *Bradley*, which was decided the following year, the Court continued to back off from its commitment to school integration. In this case, the Detroit, Michigan, school board was accused of intentional segregation in adopting policies that had resulted in a situation where by 1970 sixty-nine of the schools were 90 percent or more white and 133 schools were 90 percent or more black. The United States District Court for Eastern Michigan had ordered a multi-district integration plan that would have involved the mostly white students in the city's fifty-three suburban school districts. But the suburban areas adjacent to Detroit that didn't want to be lumped into an area-wide segregation plan that merged urban and suburban school systems appealed the lower court's decision to the Supreme Court. It ruled that the city of Detroit would have to come up with a plan for integration within the city limits.

The Court was sharply divided on this opinion. All four Nixon appointees were among the five that ruled in favor of the school board. Thurgood Marshall, William O. Douglas, William J. Brennan, and Byron R. White dissented. In his dissenting opinion, Douglas pointed out that "Metropolitan treatment of metropolitan problems is commonplace," citing sewage, water, and energy. Transportation is another. If these problems could be addressed on a multidistrict level, why not school integration? The majority's opinion in *Milliken*, coupled with that in *Rodriguez*, said Douglas, "means that there is no violation of the Equal Protection Clause though the schools are segregated by race and though the Black schools are not only 'separate' but 'inferior.' So far as equal protection is concerned we are now in a dramatic retreat from the . . . decision in 1896 [*Plessy* v. *Ferguson*] that Blacks could be segregated in public facilities provided they received equal treatment." In other words, in the two decisions, the Court had virtually approved separate but unequal schools.

14.

Late 20th Century Public Education

Since the *Milliken* case in 1974, the broad governing legal principles of school desegregation have remained substantially unchanged. During the decade of the 1970s, in some urban areas, the fight shifted away from the integration/segregation issue and focused on control of the schools. In New York City, African Americans took the lead in the fight for school decentralization, which meant taking power away from a centralized school headquarters and giving it to individual school districts.

In the same decade, the stage of the educational fight shifted back to higher education, where the Black Power movement found expression in demonstrations and demands for Black Studies departments at colleges and universities. Also on the college level, the concept of affirmative action led colleges and universities to favor similarly qualified black applicants over white wherever possible as a way to more fully integrate their student bodies and faculties.

In the 1980s, the administration of Republican president Ronald Reagan favored less big-government interference in the affairs of localities, and as part of this philosophy supported local control of schools. The Justice Department dropped a major city-suburban busing case in metropolitan Houston, Texas, and asked the courts to end supervision of desegregation plans in more than one hundred Southern districts. The Emergency School Aid Act was repealed in 1981, and the Justice Department attacked a locally designed plan in Seattle, Wash-

Students in an integrated classroom

ington, all the way to the Supreme Court, which upheld the plan. Federal research on effective school desegregation techniques was also ended, so 1986 is the last year for which statistics are available.

Based on those statistics, despite the efforts of the Reagan administration in its first six years, locally designed school integration plans had worked. All of the most integrated metropolitan areas in the nation had mandatory city-suburban busing plans of the sort from which the Supreme Court turned away in 1974. These included Louisville, Kentucky; Tampa, Florida; Wilmington, Delaware; Nashville, Tennessee; Greenville, South Carolina; and Greensboro, North Carolina. Other fairly well integrated areas were St. Louis, Missouri, and Indianapolis, Indiana (where there was one-way busing of black students from inner-city schools to the suburbs).

By the end of the 1980s, real and tangible gains had been made by many blacks who'd had the benefit of an integrated education. Evidence continued to suggest that children of all races benefited from attending integrated schools. Studies showed that black male graduates of integrated high schools were more likely to hold higher-status jobs and earn higher incomes than blacks who attended segregated schools. Forty years of efforts to integrate public education had produced a solid black middle class with the luxury to choose whether to live and go to school in integrated or segregated surroundings.

In an ironic development, some of the private academies set up by Southern whites to avoid integration in the public schools have themselves become integrated. Taken over by organizations that abolished racial restrictions, they began admitting black students. The majority of the private academies were conservative Christian schools, and black parents who sought to enroll their children wanted the discipline and the religion-based education they offered. "Parents are just looking at these schools as a place to get an education," according to Alvin Thornton, professor of political science at Howard University. "Many of them would have no knowledge of the history . . . of the school being built to keep white children from black children. They have no interest in that. The only thing they want to know is: 'I pay my tuition, can my child read and write? Is my child in what I perceive to be a safe environment where he or she has a smaller teacher-student ratio, with some Christian education?' They don't think of it in historical terms."

The residential patterns that had produced a *de facto* segregation persisted and in some regions became even more pronounced. Especially in the inner cities, a large nonwhite underclass continued to exist, trapped mostly in ghettos with no jobs and little hope. This underclass included a substantial number of African Americans whom the economic boom of the 1960s and the attitudes fostered by the civil rights movement had passed by. According to historian Roger Wilkins, "The subsequent deindustrialization and globalization of the economy meant that those who had not escaped the pull of their slave history had nothing to offer America but unskilled labor."

By the 1990s, this underclass also included a large Latino population, which in many ways suffered greater segregation than blacks. According to the 1993 study, *Status of School Desegregation, 1968–1986,* Hispanics were more likely to attend segregated schools than blacks. In the South, 77 percent of Hispanic students attended predominantly minority schools; in the North, the figure was 78 percent, and in the West, 74 percent.

By the 1990s, Americans were rethinking the ways that had been used to achieve integration of schools. In some areas where busing and other plans to achieve integration had largely worked, there was continued support for such remedies to segregation. In these localities, a majority of people believed that it is important for children to know and learn to get along with people who are not like them. There was also a great reluctance to reopen the wounds that were incurred when desegregation was first put into effect.

But in other areas, there was a determined assault on school desegregation plans, and in a number of cases these assaults were supported by the courts. In spite of the more activist stance of the administration of Democratic president Bill Clinton, at the time of the fortieth anniversary of the *Brown* decision, authorities in several cities around the nation were seeking reversals of their school busing plans, encouraged by the electoral successes of Conservative Republicans and by recent Supreme Court decisions making it easier for school districts to be released from desegregation orders. In September 1995, a federal judge declared the Denver schools sufficiently desegregated and released them from federal supervision, allowing them to end busing for racial balance. The governor of Arizona was mounting a campaign to release all the state's school districts from federal court orders. The mayor of Pittsburgh was urging the local school board to end court-ordered busing. Several school board members in Seattle, Washington, were pushing for a return to neighborhood schools. In Indianapolis, the school board voted to finance an assessment of citizens' views of the schools in anticipation of seeking an end to a fourteen-year-old busing order.

Those engaged in the retreat from past school desegregation plans included many African Americans who believed that the efforts had not worked. A disproportionate number of black students were in special education classes, were dropouts, or had failed to achieve national norms in reading and math. In some localities, black parents were calling for separate schools for young black men. Others sought an end to busing and a return to locally controlled neighborhood schools. A new doctrine of separate but equal was gaining currency, supported by many well-respected black scholars.

Whatever happens in the future, the forces of fairness and equality have achieved a victory of which they can be proud: Legal segregation, which in one form or another operated for 275 years, from the arrival of blacks in North America in 1619 through the great legal victories of the civil rights movement in the 1950s and 1960s, has been ended.

It is no small victory that the nine black stu-

For the thirtieth anniversary of the integration of Central High, the nine students met then-Governor Bill Clinton at the Governor's Mansion.

dents who first integrated Central High School in Little Rock, Arkansas, all achieved a good education and good jobs. Of the nine, only Elizabeth Eckford remained in Little Rock, where she worked as a social worker. Minnijean Brown, a writer, settled on a farm in Canada and raised six children. Ernest Green, the only one who graduated from Central, settled in New York and became a vice president at a brokerage house. Thelma Mothershed became a teacher in Illinois. Melba Patillo, after earning a graduate degree in communications from Columbia University in New York City, worked first as a television reporter and then as a communications consultant and writer in San Francisco; she married, and under her married name, Melba Patillo Beals, wrote a book about her experiences in Little Rock. Terrence Roberts earned a Ph.D. and taught on the college level in California. Jefferson Thomas worked as a Defense Department accountant in California; and Carlotta Walls worked as a realtor in Denver, Colorado.

In the fall of 1987, the nine reunited on the occasion of the thirtieth anniversary of their entry into Central High. They were greeted warmly on the front steps of the school by Arkansas governor Bill Clinton, who five years later would be elected president of the United States. The difference in attitude of the governors of the state thirty years apart was striking. But what especially impressed Melba Patillo Beals, as she wrote in her memoir, was the young black man who emerged from the front door of the school dressed in a coat and bow tie. "Good morning," he said. "I am Derrick Noble, president of the student body. Welcome to Central High."

As this book goes to press, separate but unequal schools have been unconstitutional for forty-three years. Yet, in many areas of the nation, schools remain separate and unequal. How the nation will deal with the larger issues that maintain separate but unequal schools, in fact if not by law, is a question for the future to decide.

Chronology

1861   Civil War begins

1862   President Lincoln issues Emancipation Proclamation, which takes effect January 1, 1863

1865   Civil War ends

1865   Thirteenth Amendment abolishes slavery

1865   Reconstruction begins

1868   Fourteenth Amendment guarantees civil rights to all Americans

1870   Fifteenth Amendment guarantees voting rights to all citizens

1877   Reconstruction ends

1896   *Plessy* v. *Ferguson* decision establishes doctrine of "separate but equal"

1914   World War I begins in Europe; Great Migration begins in the United States

1917   United States enters World War I

1929   Charles Hamilton Houston becomes vice dean of Howard University Law School, with a mandate to create a first-class institution

1935   National Association for the Advancement

of Colored People (NAACP) decides to launch a full-scale campaign against legal injustices suffered by African-Americans

1938 In *Gaines* v. *Missouri*, Charles Hamilton Houston successfully argues before the United States Supreme Court that the state of Missouri must either build a law school for blacks or desegregate the white one

1941 United States enters World War II

1950 Supreme Court decisions in *McLaurin* v. *Oklahoma State Regents for Higher Education* and *Sweatt* v. *Painter* establish that segregation in higher education is unconstitutional

1954 *Brown* v. *Board of Education* decision declares separate-but-equal schools unconstitutional

1955 Mrs. Rosa Parks arrested in Montgomery, Alabama; Montgomery bus boycott begins

1957 First Civil Rights Act since Reconstruction

1957 First black students enroll at Central High, Little Rock, Arkansas

1960 John F. Kennedy, a Democrat, elected president

1961 President Kennedy names Thurgood Marshall to the federal bench, the Second Circuit Court of Appeals

1963 President Kennedy assassinated in Dallas, Texas; Vice President Lyndon B. Johnson assumes the presidency

1964 Lyndon B. Johnson elected president in his own right; signs into law the Civil Rights Act of 1964, stronger than that of 1957

1965 Voting Rights Act passed

1967 Thurgood Marshall nominated by President Johnson and confirmed by the Senate to become first African-American Supreme Court Justice

1968 Lyndon B. Johnson chooses not to run for reelection as president; Richard M. Nixon, Republican of California, defeats Vice President Hubert H. Humphrey for the presidency

1969 In *Alexander* v. *Holmes County* [Mississippi] *Board of Education,* the Supreme Court ends the "all deliberate speed" timetable for integration, ruling that "the obligation of every school district is to terminate dual school systems at once and to operate now and hereafter only unitary schools"

1971 The Supreme Court rules that busing to achieve racial integration is constitutional in *Swann* v. *Charlotte-Mecklenburg* [North Carolina] *Board of Education*

1972 Congress passes the Emergency School

Aid Act, a desegregation assistance program; Richard M. Nixon reelected to the presidency

1973 In its decision in *Keyes* v. *Denver School District No. 1*, the Supreme Court finds that the Denver school board acted to intentionally segregate its system and orders it to take steps to achieve integration. Denver is the first city outside the South to implement a court-ordered busing plan

In its decision in San *Antonio Independent School District* v. *Rodriguez*, the Supreme Court upholds public school funding through property taxes, no matter that the result discriminated against poor areas

1974 President Richard Nixon resigns under threat of impeachment; Vice President Gerald R. Ford assumes the presidency

The Supreme Court's decision in *Milliken* v. *Bradley* limits crossing city-suburban boundary lines to achieve desegregation and thus drastically limits the possibility of substantial and lasting desegregation in the urban North

1976 Jimmy Carter, a Democrat from Georgia, elected president

1980 Ronald Reagan, a Republican from California, defeats Jimmy Carter for the presidency. Reagan and his administration prefer neighborhood schools and actively seek to dismantle earlier desegregation policies

The typical black student attends a school that is 36.2 percent white; the typical Hispanic student attends a school that is 35.5 percent white

1981 The 1972 Emergency School Aid Act is repealed

1986 In the last year for which federal statistics are available, school integration of whites and blacks is highest in the South, lowest in Northern and Western urban areas. Segregation of Latino students is higher in all areas where there is a heavy Latin population concentration than is segregation of African Americans

1988 Republican George Bush, vice president under Ronald Reagan, is elected to the presidency

1990–1992 In separate decisions involving Oklahoma City, Oklahoma, DeKalb County, Georgia, and Kansas City, Kansas, the Supreme Court makes it easier for school districts to be released from desegregation orders and limits their responsibilities to foster desegregation

1992 Bill Clinton, Democrat from Arkansas, is elected president; conservative Republicans win a majority of seats in Congress

1994 The typical black student attends a school that is 33.9 percent white; the typical Hispanic student attends a school that is 30.6 percent white

Between 1968 and 1994, the number of blacks in the nation's public schools grew by 178 percent and the number of Hispanics by 14 percent; the number of whites fell by 9 percent

1995 A federal district court judge releases the Denver, Colorado, public schools from federal supervision and court-ordered busing. Officials in Pittsburgh, Pennsylvania, Seattle, Washington, Indianapolis, Indiana, and elsewhere seek to end local busing plans

For Further Reading
Books for Adults

Beals, Melba Patillo. *Warriors Don't Cry: A Searing Memoir of the Battle to Integrate Little Rock's Central High*. New York: Pocket Books, a division of Simon and Schuster, 1994.

Foner, Eric. *Reconstruction: America's Unfinished Revolution, 1863–1877*. New York: Harper & Row, 1988.

Genovese, Eugene D. *Roll, Jordan, Roll: The World the Slaves Made*. New York: Vintage Books, 1976.

Kaplan, Sidney. *The Black Presence in the Era of the American Revolution, 1770–1800*. New York: New York Graphic Society, Ltd., 1973.

Kluger, Richard. *Simple Justice*. New York: Alfred A. Knopf, 1975.

McFeely, William S. *Frederick Douglass*. New York: W. W. Norton & Co., Inc., 1991.

McNeil, Genna Rae. *Groundwork: Charles Hamilton Houston and the Struggle for Civil Rights*. Philadelphia: The University of Pennsylvania Press, 1983.

For Further Reading

Orfield, Gary, et al. *Status of School Desegregation 1968–1986. A Report of the Council of Urban Boards of Education and the National School Desegregation Research Project, The University of Chicago.* Chicago, IL: 1989.

Sterling, Dorothy, ed. *Speak Out in Thunder Tones: Letters and Other Writings of Black Northerners, 1787–1865.* New York: Doubleday & Co., Inc., 1973.

———. *We Are Your Sisters: Black Women in the Nineteenth Century.* New York: W. W. Norton & Co., 1984.

Stuckey, Sterling. *Slave Culture: Nationalist Theory and the Foundations of Black America.* New York: Oxford University Press, 1987.

Tushnet, Mark V. *The NAACP's Legal Strategy Against Segregated Education, 1925–1950.* Chapel Hill, NC.: The University of North Carolina Press, 1987.

Walker, Juliet E. K. *Free Frank: A Black Pioneer on the Antebellum Frontier.* Lexington, KY: The University of Kentucky Press, 1983.

Articles

Dent, David J. "African-Americans Turning to Christian Academies," *The New York Times,* Education Life, August 4, 1996, pp. 26–28.

Wilkins, Roger. "Free at Last?" *MM,* April–May 1994, pp. 27 plus.

Books for Young Readers

Drisko, Carol F., and Edgar A. Toppin. *The Unfinished March: The History of the Negro in the United States, Reconstruction to World War I.* New York: Doubleday & Co., 1967.

Haskins, James. *Thurgood Marshall: A Life for Justice.* New York: Henry Holt & Co., 1994.

———. *Outward Dreams: Black Inventors and Their Inventions.* New York: Walker and Company, 1991.

———. *The Day Martin Luther King, Jr., Was Shot: A Photo History of the Civil Rights Movement.* New York: Scholastic Inc., 1992.

McKissack, Patricia, and Fredrick McKissack. *The Civil Rights Movement in America from 1865 to the Present.* Chicago: Children's Press, 1987.

Index

Index

Index

Index

Index

Index